SLAVERY, TERRORISM AND ISLAM

THE HISTORICAL ROOTS AND CONTEMPORARY THREAT

by Peter Hammond

FRONTLINE FELLOWSHIP

Cape Town   South Africa

Slavery, Terrorism and Islam
The Historical Roots and Contemporary Threat
by Peter Hammond

Typesetting: John Rayner
Cover Design: John Rayner

Printed in the United States of America

ISBN 9781612154985

www.xulonpress.com

SLAVERY, TERRORISM AND ISLAM

THE HISTORICAL ROOTS AND CONTEMPORARY THREAT

Revised and Expanded Third Edition

by Peter Hammond

FRONTLINE FELLOWSHIP
PO Box 74
Newlands
7725 Cape Town
South Africa
Tel: (+27-21) 689-4480
Fax: (+27-21) 689-5884
Email: admin@frontline.org.za
Web: www.frontline.org.za

Dedication

This book is dedicated to the Christians of Nigeria,
Southern Sudan and the Nuba Mountains who
have suffered such severe persecution for their faith.
In particular it is dedicated to Bishop Bullen Dolli
of Lui Diocese whose cathedral endured ten aerial
bombardments by the Sudan Air Force and whose
brother died courageously at the hands of Muslims
for refusing to renounce his faith in Christ.

Contents

Crusaders defend Acra from Muslim jihadists.

Foreword
by Dr. George Grant

The Greatest Conflict

The greatest conflict of the past century has not been between Communism and Democracy. It has not been between Liberalism and Conservatism. It has not been between Socialism and Capitalism. It has not been between Rich and Poor, Proletariat and Bourgeoisie, Industrialism and Agrarianism, Nationalism and Colonialism, Management and Labour, First World and Third World, East and West, North and South, Allied and Axis, or NATO and Soviet. All of these conflicts have been important, of course. All of them helped to define the modern era significantly. None of them should be in any way underestimated.

But while every one of these conflicts has pitted ardent foes against one another and as a result, has actually altered the course and character of recent history, none of them could be characterized as the most convulsive conflict of the past century. The most convulsive conflict of the past century, and indeed the most convulsive conflict of the past, millennium, has undoubtedly been between Islam and Civilization; it has been between Islam and Freedom; it has been between Islam and Order; it has been between Islam and Progress; it has been between Islam and Hope. While every other conflict pitting men and nations against one another has inevitably waxed and waned, this furious struggle has remained all too consistent. The tension between Islam and every aspiration and yearning of man intrudes on every issue, every discipline, every epoch, and every locale - a fact that is more evident today than perhaps ever before.

Despite this inescapable fact, most people today actually know very little about Islam. Certainly, most Christians know only the most rudimentary facts about this extraordinarily potent adversary, this extreme cultural threat to everything they hold to be good and right and true. The conflict between Islam and the rest of the world may dominate the headlines, define our foreign policy, and give new urgency to the day-to-day mission of our churches, but why that is the case, is still not very well understood.

It is for that reason that Frontline Fellowship has produced this vital new study of one of the most neglected aspects of Islam. Born out of the difficult experience of missionaries on the front lines of the battle for the soul of Africa and indeed, the world this book is designed to present the ideas, history, and aspirations of Islam through the lens of a Biblical worldview perspective. It is designed to equip ordinary Christians from every walk of life to wisely and Scripturally minster in a world where the conflict between Islam and civilization is all too obvious.

I am grateful for the commitment of Peter Hammond, and the entire team of Frontline Fellowship to make this practical and understandable study available. In this day and time we most assuredly need to understand rather than simply emote; we need to lay firm foundations rather than simply react; we need to be ready, willing, and able to present the eternal truths of Scripture in the context of the temporal realities of our poor fallen world. And that is just what this study enables us to do. May God be pleased to use it to that end and for His glory.

George Grant, PhD
Kingsmeadow

Introduction
by Rev. Fano Sibisi

Setting the Record Straight

"Slavery, Terrorism and Islam" is a well-researched account of the historical events that impact directly on present developments.

For the sake of this generation, and coming ones, someone had to do what Dr. Peter Hammond has just done; setting the record straight on the different role players in the slave trade.

It is only right that shining stars of Christianity who campaigned tirelessly for the abolition of slavery should receive their rightful place on the roll of honour. Dr. Hammond highlights the spiritual basis from which they drew their motivation.

In Muslim countries tragic stories of persecution and killing of those who dare to turn to Christ abound, yet where there is freedom of religion, Islam is driven with much fury.

In the wake of 9/11 and international acts of terrorism involving fanatical Muslim extremists, people are struggling to understand what it is in Islam that creates that kind of mentality. *"Slavery, Terrorism and Islam"* goes to the root of it all.

Christians need to take heed of Dr. Hammond's bold assertion:

"Firstly, we need to recognise that this terrorism and anti-Christian persecution is originating from the least evangelised area of the world - the Middle East. The birthplace of the Church is now the most needy mission field on earth. If we truly want to uproot the support bases of such terrorism and implode the regimes that persecute Chistians, we need to get really serious about the Great Commission of our Lord Jesus Christ. (Matthew 28:18-20)"

Impossible task?

On our own yes, but not if we are co-workers with Him who assured us that,

"All power is given unto Me in Heaven and on earth ... and, lo, I am with you always, even unto the end of the world. Amen"

Rev. Fano Sibisi
President, Christians For Truth

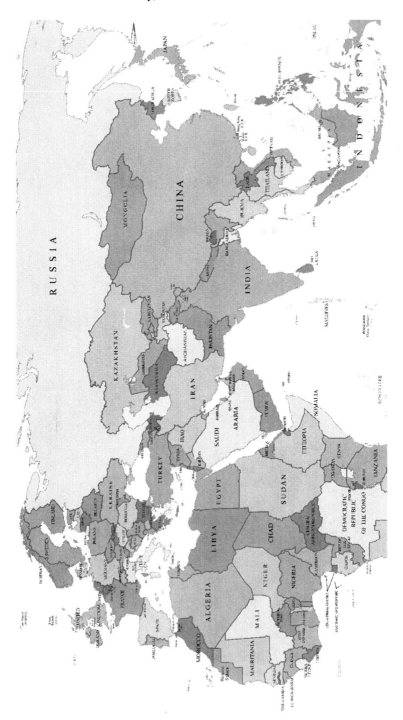

Chapter 1

The Scourge of Slavery

While much has been written concerning the Trans-Atlantic slave trade, surprisingly little attention has been given to the Islamic slave trade across the Sahara, the Red Sea and the Indian Ocean. While the European involvement in the Trans-Atlantic

Most of the slave trade has been ignored.

slave trade to the Americas lasted for just over three centuries, the Arab involvement in the slave trade has lasted fourteen centuries, and in some parts of the Muslim world is still continuing to this day.

CONTRASTS IN CAPTIVITY

A comparison of the Islamic slave trade to the American slave trade reveals some interesting contrasts. While two out of every three slaves shipped across the Atlantic were men, the proportions were reversed in the Islamic slave trade. Two women for every man were enslaved by the Muslims.

While the mortality rate for slaves being transported across the Atlantic was as high as 10%, the percentage of slaves dying in transit in the Trans Sahara and East African slave trade was between 80 and 90%!

While almost all the slaves shipped across the Atlantic were for agricultural work, most of the slaves destined for the Muslim Middle East were for sexual exploitation as concubines, in harems, and for military service.

While many children were born to slaves in the Americas, and millions of their descendants are citizens in Brazil and the USA to this day, very few descendants of the slaves that ended up in the Middle East survive.

While most slaves who went to the Americas could marry and have families, most of the male slaves destined for the Middle East slave bazaars were castrated, and most of the children born to the women were killed at birth.

It is estimated that possibly as many as 11 million Africans were transported across the Atlantic (95% of which went to South and Central America, mainly to Portuguese, Spanish and French possessions. Only 5% of the slaves went to the United States).

However, at least 28 million Africans were enslaved in the Muslim Middle East. As at least 80% of those captured by Muslim slave traders were calculated to have died before reaching the slave markets,

Over 28 million Africans have been enslaved in the Muslim world over the past 14 centuries.

it is believed that the death toll from the 14 centuries of Muslim slave raids into Africa could have been over 112 million. When added to the number of those sold in the slave markets, the total number of African victims of the Trans Saharan and East African slave trade could be significantly higher than 140 million people.

THE ABSENCE OF ARABIC ABOLITIONISTS

While Christian Reformers spearheaded the anti-slavery abolitionist movements in Europe and North America, and Great Britain mobilised her Navy, throughout most of the 19th Century, to intercept slave ships and set the captives free, there was no comparable opposition to slavery within the Muslim world.

Even after Britain outlawed the slave trade in 1807 and Europe abolished the slave trade in 1815, Muslim slave traders enslaved a further 2 million Africans. This despite vigorous British Naval activity and military intervention to limit the Islamic slave trade. By some

Every pagan civilization practised slavery.

calculations the number of victims of the 14 centuries of Islamic slave trade could exceed 180 million.

Nearly 100 years after President Abraham Lincoln issued the Emancipation Proclamation in America, and 130 years after all slaves within the British Empire were set free by parliamentary decree, Saudi Arabia and Yemen, in 1962, and Mauritania in 1980, begrudgingly removed legalised slavery from their statute books. And this only after international pressure was brought to bear. Today numerous international organisations document that slavery still continues in some Muslim countries.

THE PAGAN ORIGINS OF SLAVERY

Slavery long predated Christianity, and many of the early Christians were slaves in the Roman Empire. Without exception, the pre-Christian world accepted slavery as normal and desirable. The Greek philosopher Aristotle claimed: *"From the hour of their birth, some are marked out for subjection, others for rule."* The great civilisations of Mesopotamia, Babylon, Egypt, Greece, Rome, and all the civilisations in Central America and Africa were built upon slave labour.

English slaves in a Roman marketplace.

People became slaves by being an insolvent debtor, or by being sold into slavery by their parents, or by being born to slave parents, or by being captured in war, or through kidnapping by slave raiders and pirates. Slave dealing was an accepted way of life, fully established in all societies. Most of these slaves were white people, or Europeans. In fact the very word *"slave"*, comes from the people of Eastern Europe, the Slavs.

St. Patrick, the English missionary to the Irish, was once a slave himself, kidnapped from his home and taken to Ireland against his will. Patrick spoke out strongly against slavery. He wrote: *"But it is the women kept in slavery who suffer the most."*

Slaves at a Roman auction.

David Livingstone and his team freed slaves from Arab slave raiders in the Shire Valley.

The Greeks, from whom we derive so many modern, humanistic ideas, were utterly dependent on slavery. Even Plato's *Republic* was firmly based on slave labour. Plato said that 50 or more slaves represented the possessions of a wealthy man.

Under Roman law, when a slave owner was found murdered, all his slaves were to be executed. In one case, when a certain Pedanius Secundas was murdered, all 400 of his slaves were put to death.

Before the coming of Christ, the heathen nations despised manual work and confined it to slaves. When Christ was born, half of the population of the Roman Empire were slaves. Three quarters of the population of Athens were slaves.

Slavery was indigenous to African and Arab countries before it made its way to Europe. Slavery was widely practised by the tribes of the American Indians long before Columbus set foot on the shores of the New World. Ethiopia had slavery until 1942, Saudi Arabia until 1962, Peru until 1968, India until 1976 and Mauritania until 1980. What is also seldom remembered is that many black Americans in the 19th Century owned slaves. For example, according to the United States census of 1830, in just the one town of Charleston, South Carolina, 407 black Americans owned slaves themselves.

THE CHRISTIAN ROOTS OF LIBERTY

But Jesus revolutionised labour. By taking up the axe, the saw, the hammer and the plane, our Lord endued labour with a new dignity. Christianity undercut slavery by giving dignity to work. By reforming work, Christianity transformed the entire social order.

Our Lord Jesus Christ began His ministry in Nazareth with these words: *"The Spirit of the Lord is on Me...to proclaim freedom for the prisoners...and release to the oppressed."*

Luke 4:18

Christian Missionary David Livingstone survived numerous confrontations with slave traders.

When the apostle Paul wrote to Philemon, concerning his escaped slave, he urged him to welcome back Onesimus *"no longer as a slave, but...as a dear brother...as a man and as a brother in the Lord."* Philemon 16.

Because of these and other Scriptural commands to love our neighbour, to be a good Samaritan and to do for others what you would want them to do for you, Christians like William Wilberforce, John Newton, William Carey, David Livingstone, Lord Shaftesbury and General Charles Gordon worked tirelessly to end the slave trade, stop child labour, and set the captives free.

From the very beginning of the Christian Church, Christians freed slaves. During the 2nd and 3rd Centuries many tens of thousands of slaves were freed by people who converted to Christ. St. Melania was said to have emancipated 8,000 slaves, St. Ovidius freed 5,000, Chromatius 1,400, and Hermes 1,200. Many of the Christian clergy at Hippo under St. Augustine "freed their slaves as an act of piety." In AD315, the Emperor Constantine, just two years after he issued the edict of Milan, legalising Christianity, imposed the death penalty on those who stole children to bring them up as slaves.

The Emperor Justinian abolished all laws that prevented the freeing of slaves. St. Augustine (354 - 430) saw slavery as the product of sin and as contrary to God's Divine plan (The City of God). St. Chrysostom in the 4th Century, taught that when Christ came He annulled slavery. He proclaimed *"in Christ Jesus there is no slave...therefore it is not necessary to have a slave...buy them, and after you have taught them some skill by which they can maintain themselves, set them free."*

For centuries, throughout the Middle Ages, bishops and church councils recommended the redemption of captive slaves, and for five centuries the Trinitarian monks redeemed Christian slaves from Moorish (Muslim) servitude.

In 1102 AD, the London Church Council outlawed slavery and the slave trade. By the 12th Century slaves in Europe were rare, and by the 14th Century slavery was almost unknown on the continent of Europe.

Female slaves were captured in vast numbers for concubines in Arab harems.

Arab slave traders along the Ruvuma River, East Africa, 1866, axe a straggler.

THE ISLAMIC SLAVE TRADE

However, with the birth of Islam came a rebirth of the slave trade. As Ronald Segal in *"Islam's Black Slaves"* documents: *"When Islam conquered the Persian Sassanid Empire and much of the Byzantine Empire, including Syria and Egypt, in the 7ᵗʰ Century, it acquired immense quantities of gold…stripping churches and monasteries … either directly or by taxes, payable in gold, imposed on the clergy and looting gold from… Tombs… The state encouraged the search and sanctioned the seizure, in return for a fifth of the finds."*

Segal notes: *"Female slaves were required in considerable numbers for… musicians, singers and dancers…many more were bought for domestic workers… and many were in demand as concubines. The harems of rulers could be enormous. The harem of Abd al Rahman III (912 - 961) in Cordoba contained over 6,000 concubines! And the one in the Fatimid Palace in Cairo had twice as many…"*

Islam's Black Slaves also reveals that the castration of male slaves was commonplace. *"The Calipha in Baghdad at the beginning of the 10th Century had 7,000 black eunuchs and 4,000 white eunuchs in his palace."* It was noted that there were widespread *"homosexual relations"* as well. *Islam's Black Slaves* notes that Islamic teachers throughout the centuries consistently

Many millions of Africans died en route to the slave bazaars of the Middle East.

defended slavery: *"For there must be masters and slaves."* Others noted that blacks *"lack self-control and steadiness of mind and they are overcome by fickleness, foolishness and ignorance. Such are the blacks who live in the extremity of the land of Ethiopia, the Nubians, Zanj and the like."*

Ibn Khaldun (1332 - 1406) the pre-eminent Islamic medieval historian and social thinker wrote: *"The Negro nations are as a rule submissive to slavery...because they have attributes that are quite similar to dumb animals."*

By the Middle Ages, the Arab word *"abd"* was in general use to denote a black slave while the word *"mamluk"* referred to a white slave. Even as late as the 19ᵗʰ Century, it was noted that in Mecca *"there are few families...that do not keep slaves...they all keep mistresses in common with their lawful wives."*

It was noted that black slaves were castrated *"based on the assumption that the blacks had an ungovernable sexual appetite."*

Ibn Timiyya wrote:" Slavery is justified because of the war itself; however it is not permissible to enslave a free Muslim. It is lawful to kill the infidel or to enslave him, and it also makes it lawful to take his offspring into captivity."

When the Fatimids came to power they slaughtered all the tens of thousands of black military slaves and raised an entirely new slave army. Some of these slaves were conscripted into the army at age ten. From Persia to Egypt to Morocco, slave armies from 30,000 to up to 250,000 became common-place.

Even Ronald Segal, who is most sympathetic to Islam and clearly prejudiced against Christianity, admits that well over 30 million black Africans would have died at the hands of Muslim slave traders or ended up in Islamic slavery. The Islamic slave trade took place across the Sahara Desert, from the coast of the Red Sea, and from East Africa across the Indian Ocean. The Trans-Sahara trade was conducted along six major slave routes. Just in the 19th Century, for which we have more accurate records, 1.2 million slaves were brought across the Sahara into the Middle East,

About 80% of those captured by Muslim slave raiders in Africa died before reaching the slave markets.

450,000 down the Red Sea and 442,000 from East African coastal ports. That is a total of 2 million black slaves - just in the 1800s. At least 8 million more were calculated to have died before reaching the Muslim slave markets.

Islam's Black Slaves records: *"In the 1570's, a Frenchman visiting Egypt found many thousands of blacks on sale in Cairo on market days. In 1665 Father Antonios Gonzalis, a Spanish/Belgian traveller, reported 800 - 1,000 slaves on sale in the Cairo market on a single day. In 1796, a British traveller reported a caravan of 5,000 slaves departing from Darfur. In 1838, it was estimated that 10,000 to 12,000 slaves were arriving in Cairo each year."* Just in the Arabic plantations off the East Coast of Africa, on the islands of Zanzibar and Pemba, there were 769,000 black slaves.

In the 19th Century, the East African black slave trade included 347,000 slaves shipped to Arabia, Persia and India; 95,000 slaves were shipped to the Arab plantations in the Mascareme Islands.

Segal notes *"The high death rate and low birth rate among black slaves in the Middle East and the astonishingly low birth rate amongst black slave women"* in North Africa and the Middle East. *"Islamic civilisation…lagged increasingly behind the West in protecting public health. The arithmetic of the Islamic black slave trade must also not ignore the lives of those men, women and children taken or lost during the procurement, storage and transport…the sale of a single captive for slavery might represent a loss of ten in the population from defenders killed in attacks on villages, the deaths of women and children from related famine and the loss of children, the old and the sick, unable to keep up with their captors or killed along the way in hostile encounters, or dying of sheer misery."*

One British explorer encountered over 100 human skeletons from a slave caravan en route to Tripoli.

The explorer Heinrich Barth recorded that a slave caravan lost 40 slaves in the course of a single night at Benghazi.

The British explorer Richard Lander came across a group of 30 slaves in West Africa, all of them stricken with smallpox, all bound neck to neck with twisted strips of bullock hide.

One caravan with 3,000 proceeding from the coast in East Africa lost two thirds of its number from starvation, disease and murder.

In the Nubian desert, one slave caravan of 2,000 slaves literally vanished as every slave died.

AN EYEWITNESS ACCOUNT

In 1818, Captain Lyon of the Royal Navy reported that the Al-Mukani in Tripoli *"waged war on all its defenceless neighbours and annually carried off 4,000 to 5,000 slaves…a piteous spectacle! These poor oppressed beings were, many of them, so exhausted as to be scarcely able to walk, their legs and feet were much swelled, and by their enormous size formed a striking contrast with their emaciated bodies. They were all borne down with loads of firewood, and even poor little children, worn to skeletons by fatigue and hardships, were obliged to bear their burden, while many of their inhuman masters with dreadful whip suspended from their waist…all the traders speak of slaves as farmers do of cattle…the defenceless state of the Negro kingdoms to the southward are temptations too strong to be resisted, a force is therefore annually sent…to pillage these defenceless people, to carry them off as slaves, burn their towns, kill the aged and infants, destroy their crops and inflict on them every possible misery…all slavery is for an unlimited time…none of their owners ever moved without their whips - which were in constant use…drinking too much water, bringing too little wood or falling asleep before the cooking was finished, were considered nearly capital crimes, and it was in vain for these poor creatures to plead the excuse of being tired. Nothing could withhold the application of the whip. No slaves dared to be ill or unable to walk, but when the poor sufferer dies, the master suspects that there must have been something 'wrong inside' and regrets not having liberally applied their usual remedy of burning the belly with a red-hot iron."*

Records for Morocco in 1876 show that market prices for slaves varied from £10 ($48) to £30 ($140). Female slaves comprised the vast majority of sales with "attractive virgins" fetching between £40 to £80 ($192 - $386). It was reported that *"a considerable majority of the slaves crossing the Sahara were destined to become concubines in North Africa, the Middle East and occasionally even further afield."*

CHRISTIAN SLAVES - MUSLIM MASTERS

Segal also observed that: *"White slaves from Christian Spain, Central and Eastern Europe"* were also shipped into the Middle East and served in the *"palaces of rulers and the establishments of the rich."* He records that: *"All slavic eunuchs…are castrated in that region and the operation is performed by Jewish merchants."*

Arab sultans could have thousands of eunuchs and concubines.

Serge Trifkovic in The Sword of the Prophet notes that in 781AD over 7,000 Greeks were enslaved by the Muslims after

Muslim slave raiders kidnapped hundreds of thousands of women from Europe for harems in the Middle East.

they conquered Ephesus. When the Muslims captured Thessalonica in 903AD over 22,000 Christians were sold into slavery. Similarly in 1064 when Muslims invaded Georgia and Armenia.

Historian Otto Scott in his book *"The Great Christian Revolution"* details how Suleiman and his Turkish army of 300,000 invaded Hungary in 1526 and carried off 200,000 Hungarian Christians into slavery. In 1571 thousands of Greeks on Cyprus were shipped to Constantinople as slaves.

Historian Robert Davis in his book *"Christian Slaves, Muslim Masters - White Slavery in the Mediterranean, the Barbary Coast and Italy"*, estimates that North African Muslim pirates abducted and enslaved more than 1 million Europeans between 1530 and 1780. These white Christians were seized in a series of raids which depopulated coastal towns from Sicily to Cornwall. Thousands of white Christians in coastal areas were seized every year to work as galley slaves, labourers and concubines for Muslim slave masters in what is today Morocco, Tunisia, Algeria and Libya. Villages and towns on the coast of Italy, Spain, Portugal and France were the hardest hit, but the Muslim slave raiders also seized people as far afield as Britain, Ireland and Iceland. They even captured 130 American seamen from ships they boarded in the Atlantic between 1785 and 1793.

According to one report, 7,000 English people were abducted between 1622 to 1644, many of them ship crews and passengers. But the Corsairs also landed on unguarded beaches, often at night, to snatch the unwary. Almost all the inhabitants of the village of Baltimore, in

More than a million Christian Europeans were enslaved by Muslim pirates.

Ireland, were captured in 1631, and there were other raids in Devon and Cornwall. Many of these white, Christian slaves were put to work in quarries, building sites and galleys and endured malnutrition, disease and mistreatment at the hands of their Muslim slave masters. Many of them were used for public works such as building harbours.

The Slave Market at Omduruman in Sudan.

As the Ottoman empire's ruling class degenerated into sensual overload, many of the intelligent kidnapped Christian boys from Europe came to play an increasingly important role as tutors, advisors, engineers and even managers.

Female captives were sexually abused in palace harems and others were held as hostages and bargained for ransom. *"The most unlucky ended up stuck and forgotten out in the desert, in some sleepy town such as Suez, or in Turkish*

Sultanate galleys, where some slaves rowed for decades without ever setting foot on shore." Professor Davis estimates that up to 1.25 million Europeans were enslaved by Muslim slave raiders between 1500 to 1800.

THE EUROPEAN SLAVE TRADE

While Islam dominated the slave trade from the 7th to the 15th Century, between 1519 and 1815 Europe also joined in this trade in human flesh. And it was those European nations which had suffered the most at the hands of Muslim slave raiders, and under centuries of Muslim military occupation, Spain and Portugal, who dominated the European slave trade.

It was the enemies of the Reformation who brought Europe into this disgraceful trade. It was Emperor Charles V (whom Martin Luther defied with his historic *"My conscience is captive to the Word of God...here I stand I can do no other..."* speech) of the Holy Roman Empire who first authorised Europe's involvement in the slave trade in 1519. Because of Pope Alexander VI's Line of Demarcation Bill of 1493 which barred Spain from Africa, Spain issued Asientos (a monopoly) to other nations to supply slaves for her South American colonies. First Portugal had this lucrative franchise, then the Dutch, then the French. Finally, by the treaty of Utrecht 1713, the *Asientos* was transferred from France to Britain. Britain's involvement in slavery was first authorised in 1631 by King Charles I (who was later executed by Parliament). His son, Charles II, reintroduced it by Royal Charter in 1672.

According to *"The Slave Trade"* by Hugh Thomas, approximately 4 million (35.4%) went to Portuguese controlled Brazil; 2.5 million (22.1%) to the Spanish nations of South and Central America; 2 million (17.7%)

to the British West Indies (mostly Jamaica); 1.6 million (14.1%) to French West Indies; half a million (4.4%) to Dutch West Indies and half a million (4.4%) to North America.

THE AMERICAN SLAVE TRADE

It is extraordinary that, considering that less than 5% of all the Trans-Atlantic slaves ended up in North America, the vast majority of films, books and articles concerning the slave trade concentrate only on the American involvement in the slave trade, as though slavery was a uniquely American aberration. However, the vastly greater involvement of Portugal, Spain and France seems to be largely ignored. Even more so the far greater and longer-running Islamic slave trade into the Middle East has been so ignored as to make it one of history's best-kept secrets.

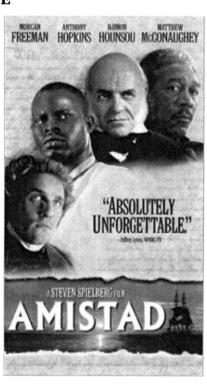

We tend to focus on what happened in North America because the United States would eventually fight a war, in part over slavery, and because of the enormous and vocal American opposition to slavery. This was in sharp contrast to the indifference that Muslims, Africans and many Europeans evidenced towards it.

THE AFRICAN SLAVE TRADE

The legends of European slave raiders venturing into the jungles of Africa to capture free peoples are generally just that: myths.

Slave trading in Africa was practiced between the tribes long before the Muslim slave traders came.

The embarrassing fact of history is that the Europeans did not have to use any force to obtain these slaves. The slaves were *"sold"* by their black owners. There was no need for the slave raiders to risk their lives or venture into the jungles of Africa; they simply purchased the people from African chiefs and Muslim slave traders at the coast.

However, while the slave trade and slavery itself was always criticised vigorously in Britain and America, no comparable criticism was evident in the Muslim Middle East or amongst the African tribes which sold their own people, and neighbouring tribes, into slavery. Almost all of the African slaves transported across the Atlantic were captured and sold by African rulers and merchants.

Every year, for about 600 years the Kingdom of Nubia (in present day Sudan) was forced to send a tribute of slaves to the Muslim sultans in Cairo.

Many chiefs found it more profitable to sell their enemies, criminals and debtors than to kill or imprison them. Many were weaker neighbouring tribes conquered for the express purpose of selling their people into slavery. The disgraceful fact is that there were three equally guilty partners in the crime of the Trans Atlantic slave trade: pagan African chiefs, Muslim Arabs and Christian Europeans.

The Trade, as it became known, involved a triangular voyage. Slave ships sailed from Bristol or Liverpool loaded with cloths, beads, muskets, iron bars and brandy. This merchandise was then traded in West Africa in exchange for slaves. Mostly African chiefs sold their own people, or engaged in wars and slave raids against neighbouring tribes

Many African chiefs sold their enemies, criminals or debtors as slaves – or raided weaker neighbouring tribes.

to capture victims for this trade. Often professional Arab slave traders provided the victims.

The middle passage transported the slaves to the West Indies. Here the slaves were sold and the ships loaded with spices, rum, molasses and sugar. The third leg of the journey was the return to England. The average Englishman on the street was kept in the dark as to what was actually happening on the middle passage, until, in 1785, Thomas Clarkson's landmark study *"Slavery and Commerce In the Human Species"* was first published at Cambridge. According to Clarkson's research, 10% of the slaves would normally die during the middle passage. Strong men would fetch as much as £40 while the women and children were sold in cheap batches with the sick and weak men. In England 18,000 people were employed simply in making the goods to trade for slaves in Africa. This trade constituted 4.4% of British exports.

WILBERFORCE'S WAR

On Sunday 28 October 1787, William Wilberforce wrote in his diary: *"God Almighty has set before me two great objects, the suppression of the slave trade*

In 1807 the British Parliament voted to outlaw the slave trade.

and the Reformation of society." For the rest of his life, William Wilberforce dedicated his life as a Member of Parliament to opposing the slave trade and working for the abolition of slavery throughout the British Empire.

On 22 February 1807, twenty years after he first began his crusade, and in the middle of Britain's war with France, Wilberforce and his team's labours were rewarded with victory. By an overwhelming 283 votes for to 16 against, the motion to abolish the slave trade was carried in the House of Commons. The parliamentarians leapt to their feet with great cheers and gave Wilberforce the greatest and most emotional ovation ever seen in British history. William bent forward in his seat, his head in his hands, tears of gratitude streaming down his face.

In 1809, the British government mobilised its Navy to search suspected slave ships, even foreign vessels on the high seas. In 1810, the British Parliament declared slave trading a felony, punishable by fourteen years hard labour. In 1814, the British representative at the Congress of Vienna insisted on the abolition of the slave trade being included in the International Treaty. This Treaty was signed by all the European powers on 9 June 1815. In 1825, Britain passed a bill making slave trading punishable by death.

Finally, just three days before William Wilberforce died, by an Act of Parliament in 1833, the British abolished slavery itself - setting all 700,000 slaves in British overseas territories free. Wilberforce's lifetime campaign of 46 years was now fully successful. *"Thank God that I've lived to witness the day in which England is willing to give 20 million pounds sterling for the abolition of slavery!"* he exclaimed. Within

William Wilberforce led the campaign against slavery for 46 years.

three days he died rejoicing. (For the story of how slavery was abolished see the chapter on William Wilberforce - Missionary to Parliament in *The Greatest Century of Missions*).

The *"History of European Morals"* suggests that *"the unweary, unostentatious and glorious crusade of England against slavery may probably be regarded as among the three or four perfectly virtuous pages comprised in the history of nations."*

The abolition of slavery was one of the great turning points in history. And the long and vigorous crusade by the British Navy throughout the 19th Century against the slave trade ranks as one of the most extraordinary and unselfish applications of national policy ever seen in the history of nations.

"...where the Spirit of the Lord is, there is liberty."

2 Corinthians 3:17

SET FREE TO SERVE CHRIST

One of the many fruits of William Wilberforce's life long crusade against the slave trade was that Samuel Ajayi Crowther, who was born in 1807 (the year Great Britain abolished the slave trade) in Yorubaland

All slaves in the British Empire were set free by Parliamentary decree, in 1833.

Rescued from slavery by the British Navy, Samuel Crowther became the first African bishop of the Church of England.

(modern Western Nigeria) was rescued by a British naval squadron. When Samuel was just thirteen years old, he was captured by slave traders for transport across the Atlantic, but was rescued by the Navy. Samuel received an education in Sierra Leone, where he was converted to Christ, and after further education in England he was ordained as a minister of the Church of England for service with the Church Missionary Society.

Samuel participated in the expedition up the Niger River Valley to overcome the ravages of the slave industry still entrenched there. Of the 145 Europeans on that expedition, 130 were struck down with Malaria, and 40 died. Yet the expedition succeeded in establishing a Missionary Center at Fourah Bay for training liberated slaves to evangelise West Africa. It was built on the very place where a slave market had once stood. The rafters of the roof were made almost entirely from the masts of old slave ships.

Samuel Crowther was one of the first four students to graduate from Fourah Bay's College, Sub-Saharan Africa's first university. In 1864, Samuel Crowther was ordained as the first African Bishop of the Church of England in an overflowing Canterbury cathedral. Today there are eighteen times more Anglicans worshipping in church every Sunday in Nigeria than there are in Great Britain.

LIVINGSTONE'S TRAVELS

However, as the British Navy was defeating the slave trade in the Atlantic, the East African slave trade was increasing. It was missionary explorer David Livingstone whose graphic descriptions brought the ravages of the East African slave trade to light. His *Missionary Travels* and *Narrative of an Expedition to the Zambezi* exposed the horrors of the slave trade: *"Two of the women had been shot the day before for attempting to untie their thongs. One woman had her infant's brains knocked out because she could not carry her load and it; and a man was dispatched with an axe because he had broken down with fatigue… those taken out of the country are but a very small section of the sufferers. We never realised the atrocious nature of the traffic until we saw it at the fountain head. 'There truly Satan has his seat.' Besides those actually captured, thousands are killed and die of their wounds and famine, driven from their villages by the internecine war waged for slaves with their own clansmen and neighbours, slain by the lust of gain, which is stimulated, be it remembered always, by the slave purchases of Cuba and elsewhere."*

Missionary David Livingstone confronted Muslim slave traders and secured the freedom of thousands of slaves.

The slave market in Zanzibar sold an average of 300 slaves every day.

A TRADE IN HUMAN MISERY

The British and Foreign Anti-Slavery Society reported that most slaves were captured in the Lake Nyassa area (Malawi and Mozambique), the Bahr El Ghazal region and in areas of Ethiopia. Slaves were taken to East African markets like Zanzibar, Kilwa and Quelimane and then shipped to Turkey, India, Saudi Arabia, Yemen, Oman, Iraq, Iran and to the islands of Pemba, Reunion and Madagascar.

Muslim slave owners were entitled by Sharia law to sexually exploit their slaves

The *Anti-Slavery Reporter* estimated the Muslim slave trade as exporting 63,000 slaves per year. Some estimates went as high as 500,000 slaves exported in a single year. One researcher, Ralph Austen calculated that between 1830 and 1861 imports of slaves to the Persian Gulf averaged 3,400 per annum. This same researcher noted that an average of 8,855 slaves a year were retained as slaves on the East African coast as slaves of African slave masters.

Few authors dared describe the horrors involved in the Trans- Sahara slave trade: kidnapping and castrating young boys to be sold as eunuchs *("the living dead")* in the homes of wealthy Arab landlords and force marching young women across endless miles of

Muslim slavers routinely castrated male slaves.

scorching sand in the Sahara desert to become slave concubines, most dying in transit. The Muslim slave trade typically dealt in the sale of castrated male slaves: eunuchs. Eunuchs were created by completely amputating the scrotum and penis of eight to twelve year old African boys. Hundreds of thousands of young boys bled to death during this gory procedure. The survival rate from this process was horrific. These castrated boys brought the highest price at the slave market.

SHARIA LAW AND SLAVERY

Islam's Black Slaves notes: *"the Quran stipulated that female slaves might lawfully be enjoyed by their masters."* *Muhammad* himself owned many slaves, some of whom he captured in wars of conquest and some he purchased. The names of forty slaves owned by Muhammad are recorded by Muslim chroniclers. Islamic law (Sharia) contains elaborate regulations for slavery. A slave had no right to be heard in court (testimony was forbidden by slaves), slaves had no right to property, could marry only with the permission of the owner, and were considered to be chattel, that is the movable property, of the slave owner. Muslim slave owners were specifically entitled by Sharia law to sexually exploit their slaves, including hiring them out as prostitutes.

A dhow, the favourite slave carrying vessel of Arab slave traders.

Arab traders beat their cargo into submission on the run from the African coast to Zanzibar.

The Hadith states: *"No Muslim should be killed for killing a non-Muslim, nor a freeman for a slave."*

One reason why very little has been written about the Arab involvement in slavery is that traditional Islamic culture still condones slavery. The Sharia, the codified Islamic law which is based upon the teachings and example of Muhammad, contains explicit regulations for slavery. One of the primary principles of Islam is following the example of Muhammad. Whatever Muhammad did, we must do, what he forbade, we

British explorers set the captives free.

British troops attack a slave trade stockade on Zanzibar.

A steam pinnache of HMS London puts a warning shot across the bow of a slaving dhow in 1881.

Slaves set free by the British Navy.

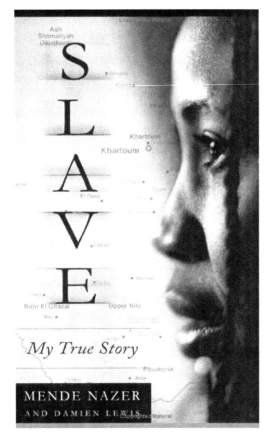

My True Story

MENDE NAZER
AND DAMIEN LEWIS

must forbid, what he did not forbid, we may not forbid. As Muhammad himself traded in slaves and owned slaves, accumulating multiple wives, even marrying a six year old, and having concubines - slavery and the sexual exploitation of women is deeply ingrained in Islamic tradition. Muslim nations had engaged in the slave trade for over 600 years before Europe became involved in the Trans-Atlantic slave trade.

SLAVERY TODAY

Almost 200 years after the British outlawed the slave trade in 1807, slave raids and the sale of slaves in Muslim markets continues in countries like Sudan. The slave trade remained legal in Saudi Arabia until 1962, when under international pressure it was finally abolished. However, there are persistent, credible reports, that slavery persists in Mauritania, Libya, Saudi Arabia, and even that slaves from Sudan are ending up in Saudi Arabia.

Recently, a former slave from the Nuba Mountains of Sudan, Mende Nazer, had her autobiography: *"Slave: My True Story"* published. Mende was captured in 1992, she was first a slave to a rich Arab family in Khartoum, and then in 2002 to a Sudanese diplomat in London, from whom she escaped and sought political asylum.

THE LAW OF LIBERTY

Although the Old Testament provided for slavery for criminals and insolvent debtors, kidnapping and enslaving law-abiding people incurred the death penalty. *"He who kidnaps a man and sells him, or if he is found in his hand, shall surely be put to death."* Exodus 21:16

Logo of the British and Foreign Anti-Slavery Society.

The New Testament expressly forbids both the slave trade and slavery itself. *"...the Law is made not for the righteous but for Law breakers...for those who kill their fathers or mothers, for murderers, for adulterers and perverts, for **slave traders** and liars and perjurers..."* 1 Timothy 1:9-10

"There is neither Jew nor Greek, slave nor free...for you are all one in Christ Jesus." Galatians 3:28

"From one man He made every nation of men..." Acts 17:26

"Love the Lord your God with all your heart, with all your soul and with all your mind and with all your strength... love your neighbour as yourself." Mark 12:30-31

"Then you will know the truth and the truth will set you free." John 8:32

"...where the Spirit of the Lord is, there is freedom." 2 Corinthians 3:17

"...proclaim liberty throughout the land..." Leviticus 25:10

"Justice lifts the nations." This oil painting hangs in the Palace of Justice in Lausanne, Switzerland.

Chapter 2

Uprooting Terrorism

t is no accident that the most vicious terrorism originates from the least evangelised area of the world. The Muslim Middle East represents the most complex political challenge and potentially an enormous military threat to the free world. It is also the greatest missionary challenge to the Christian Church.

Muslim states are the most severe persecutors of Christians. And radical Muslim extremists are the most vicious terrorists, hijackers, kidnappers, suicide bombers and assassins. **The failure of the Christian Church to fulfill the Great Commission in the Middle East continues to have far-reaching and disastrous consequences.**

Islam is a challenge that we cannot ignore. However, very few Christians understand Islam or know how to respond to it.

TERRORISM'S MISSIONARY VISION

The primary suspect for the multiple, co-ordinated terrorist attacks on the United States, Osama Bin Laden, aside from his extensive business and terrorist connections, has also been a major sponsor of Islamic missionary activity. Bin Laden has been a financial contributor to the Islamic Propagation Centre International, based in Durban, South Africa. I have visited the IPCI on numerous occasions and debated

these Muslim extremists in the biggest Mosque in the Southern Hemisphere. The IPCI credited Bin Laden with personally financing the translation of the Qur'an into Zulu. He has been known to make donations of up to $1,000,000 at a time to the IPCI.

Clearly Bin Laden is a radical Islamicist with a broad strategy and a world vision. His hatred for America is apparently more religiously motivated than political. Although many would see America as a secular country with a large number of Christians, to radical Islamicists like Bin Laden, America is the largest and strongest Christian nation on earth and the primary supporter of Christian missions worldwide. By striking at the financial centre of America, one of his aims could have been to cause a drop in support for Christian missions – even as he helps finance a massive continent wide Islamic offensive to turn Africa into a Muslim continent.

A GLOBAL AGENDA

The multi-national Al-Qa'ida organisation set up by Bin Laden during the time he was based in Sudan (1991–1996) seeks the *"global radicalization of existing Islamic groups and the creation of radical Islamic groups where none existed. Al-Qa'ida supports Muslim fighters in Afghanistan, Bosnia, Chechnya, Tajikistan, Somalia, Yemen and now Kosovo. It also trains members of terrorist organisations from … Philippines, Algeria and Eritrea. Al-Qa'ida's goal is to unite all Muslims and to establish a government which follows the rule of the Caliphas … by force … to overthrow nearly all Muslim governments, which are … corrupt, to drive Western influence from those countries, and eventually to abolish state boundaries."* (Al-Qa'ida, FAS 17/9/01)

"AFRICA FOR ISLAM"

In October 1995 Muammar Gaddafi hosted a two-week conference in Tripoli, which was attended by Muslim leaders from 80 countries. At this Muslim Leaders Conference, strategies to transform Africa into an Islamic continent were discussed.

Participants openly admitted that their goals were to make **Arabic** the official language of the continent and **Islam** the official religion. One South African member of Parliament, Farouk Cassim, declared: *"It will probably be the biggest revolution to sweep Africa."* The head of the Islamic Propagation Centre International (IPCI) at that time, Yousuf Deedat, announced afterwards that South Africa was high on the

A Frontline Fellowship group debates an Imam in a mosque.

Most of the villages and churches in the Nuba Mountains were destroyed by the National Islamic Front government's scorched earth policy.

agenda of the Islamic offensive: *"We are going to turn South Africa into a Muslim state. We have the money to do it,"* he said (Sunday Times, 22/10/95). At present, less than 2% of South Africans are Muslims. About 40% of the population of Africa are Muslims. 17 of the 55 countries in Africa are officially Islamic states.

UNDERSTANDING JIHAD

What few Westerners understand is that Muslim leaders who call for the overthrow of all governments and the establishment of an Islamic superstate controlling all aspects of life, for every person on earth, are not necessarily extremists on the fringe of Islam. Jihad, the subjugation and forcible conversion of all people to Islam and world domination are, in fact, central tenants of Islam. *Jihad* is **the sixth pillar of Islam.**

Jihad was so important to Muhammad that he declared it to be **the second most important deed in Islam.** *"Allah's apostle was asked, 'What is the best deed?' He replied, 'To believe in Allah and his apostle.' The questioner then asked, 'What is the next (in goodness)?' He replied, **'To participate in Jihad** (religious fighting) in Allah's cause.'"* – The Hadith, Al Bukhari, Vol. 1 no 25.

Now, of course, most Muslims are neither terrorists nor terrorist sympathisers. While many Muslims publicly rejoiced over the news of the horrific terrorist attacks on New York and Washington D.C., most did not. We need to be careful not to blame all Muslims for what certain individuals do in the name of Islam. Of course, those peace-loving, law-abiding Muslims are not being consistent with the Jihad teachings of the Quran. They are probably more influenced by the Christian ideal of loving your neighbour than the Islamic doctrine of Jihad.

QURANIC ROOTS OF JIHAD

In fact, Muslims are often allies of Christians in the campaigns against gambling, pornography, homosexuality, abortion, evolutionism and atheism. Muslims and Christians also agree that God is both the Creator and the eternal Judge of the whole world and everyone in it.

However, it is important for us to recognise the Quranic roots which are quoted by the Muslim terrorists to support their atrocities. If this violent position does not represent mainstream Islam, Muslim leaders must clearly denounce the literal application of these Jihad verses and declare apostate all Muslims who resort to terrorism as murderers destined to an eternity in hell.

The Quran teaches that Muslims are superior to all others: *"Ye (Muslims) are the best of peoples evolved for mankind ..."* Surah 3:110. Muslims are forbidden to befriend Jews or Christians. *"O ye who believe! Take not the Jews and the Christians for your friends and protectors. They are but friends and protectors to each other. And he amongst you that turns to them (for friendship) is one of them ..."* Surah 5:54

Islam instructs its adherents to fight until all their opponents submit. Christians and Jews may be spared if they pay *"Jizya"* – a penalty tax – with willing submission. *"Fight those who believe not in God nor the last day ... Nor acknowledge the religion of truth, (even if they are) of the people of the Book, until they pay Jizya (tribute taxes) with willing submission, and feel themselves subdued."* Surah 9:29

The Bible declares "How beautiful on the mountains are the feet of those who bring good news ..." Is 52:7. Because of Sharia law this man no longer has any feet, they have been axed off, but he still travels by donkey or "walks" on his knees to spread the Gospel.

"Fight and slay the pagans wherever ye find them and seize them, beleaguer them, and lie in wait (ambush) for them in every strategem (of war)." Surah 9:5 (also 2:193)

"Therefore, when ye meet the unbelievers (in fight), smite at their necks; at length, when ye have thoroughly subdued them, bind a bond firmly (on them); thereafter (is the time for) either generosity or ransom: until the war lays down its burdens, thus (are ye commanded)". Surah 47:4

There are at least 109 Jihad verses in the Quran.

For those who resist Islam – execution or mutilation is decreed: *"The punishment of those who wage war against Allah and his apostle, and strive with might and main for mischief through the land is: execution or crucifixion, or the cutting off the hands and feet from opposite sides or exile from the land ..."* Surah 5:36

Now, all of these texts appear to be contradicted by Surah 2:256, which states: *"Let there be no compulsion in religion."* But there seems a clear break between the early Muhammad, and the later Muhammad. The early Muhammad was married to only one wife, Khadeja, courageously spoke out against idolatry and polytheism in Mecca and encouraged friendship with the Christians. The later Muhammad, after the death of his first wife and flight to Medina, accumulated at least 15 more wives, including 9 year old Aisha, started raiding caravans, massacred 600 Jews for failing to acknowledge him as the prophet, and propagated the doctrine of Jihad. In a sense, there are two Muhammad's and two Qurans. The early pre-Medina Surahs demonstrate tolerance and respect for Christians, whereas the later Surahs unleashed Jihad.

THE BENEFITS OF JIHAD

In the *Mishkat* the rewards for participation in Jihad are spelled out: *"the Messenger of Allah said: To, whichever village you go … its one fifth is for Allah and his Messenger and the remainder is for you."* (Mishkat II, page 412).

" … *the soldiers of Islam fought tooth and nail. They would get Paradise in case of death in a holy war, and booty in case of conquest, Jihad is therefore the best source of all acquisitions."* (Mishkat II, page 440).

"Jihad is one of the chief meritorious acts in the eye of Islam and it is the best source of earnings." (Mishkat II, page 340).

"This is the best method of earning both spiritual and temporal. If victory is won, there is enormous booty and conquest of a country, which cannot be equalled to any other source of earning. If there is defeat or death, there is everlasting Paradise and a great spiritual benefit. This sort of Jihad is conditional upon pure motive, i.e. for establishing the kingdom of Allah on earth." (Mishkat II, page 253).

In the Hadith, Muhammad is quoted as decreeing that Muslims may not be punished for killing a non-Muslim: ***"No Muslims should be killed for killing a kafir (infidel)."*** (vol. 9:50)

Those who die in holy war are guaranteed to go to Heaven. *"The person who participates in Jihad (Holy battles) in Allah's cause and nothing compels him to do so except belief in Allah and his apostle, will be recompensed by Allah either with a reward or booty (if he survives) or will be admitted to paradise (if he is killed)."* (vol. 1:35)

Violent words that are accompanied by violent actions cannot be dismissed as merely symbolic. Muhammad engaged in 47 battles, ambushes and raids on merchant caravans in his lifetime. The Hadith names 27 individuals

who were assassinated on Muhammad's words and over 600 Jewish men who were beheaded for refusing to accept Muhammad as a true prophet.

Many assume that the concept of Jihad, or holy war, is an aberration not truly representative of Islam. Some leaders have stated that *"Islam teaches a God of love just like Christianity and Judaism"* and *"no religion condones violence or terrorism."* Unfortunately that is not true. Islam is no ordinary religion.

"There is a way which seemeth right unto a man, but the ends thereof are the ways of death."   Proverbs 14:12

SHARIA AND THE HOUSE OF WAR

Islam divides the world into two sectors: *Dar-al-Islam* (the House of Islam) and *Dar-al-Harb* (The House of War). The only countries considered to be at peace are those where Islamic law *(the Sharia)* is enforced. All other countries, as part of Dar-al-Harb, are considered legitimate targets.

It is significant that the calendar of Islam does not begin with the birth of Muhammad, nor the onset of his *"revelations"*, nor the assembling of the first Muslim community, nor the flight of Muslim refugees to Abyssinia. The 12 years of persecution in Mecca were not

An Mi-24 Hind helicopter of the Sudan Air Force strafing Christians in the Nuba Mountains of Sudan.

considered the start of their new religion. The Muslim calendar only begins when Islam became a political state, under Sharia Law, in Medina. The scenes of Muslims pressing their foreheads to the ground outside Mosques are not indications of a spiritual discipline as much as an aggressive political statement.

Islam in Arabic means submission, surrender or subjugation. A *Muslim* is one who submits. The Arabic word for peace is *Salam*. *Islam* is the active form of *Salam*. Muslims see themselves as a *"peace-making force"* using argument, intrigue, commerce, threats, terrorism, warfare and every

Muslims are involved in 90% of the wars in the world today.

other means possible to secure Islam as the only religion worldwide.

"And fight them on until there is no more tumult or oppression, and there prevails justice and faith in Allah altogether and everywhere." Surah 8:39

In the light of these teachings, it should be no surprise to learn that since 1948, the 21 Arab countries have suffered 30 wars, 63 successful revolutions, at least 75 unsuccessful revolutions, and the murder of 36 heads of state. In the Arab world, revolutions and assassinations have been the most prevalent means of political expression and attaining power. One out of every three barrels of oil sold by the Mideast has gone to pay for weapons.

THE MANY FACES OF JIHAD

It may be hard for Christians to understand the concept of such a militant religion, but the primary aim of Islam is not spiritual but political. (One exception to this could be the Sufis – mystical Muslims who re-interpret these Jihad passages to apply to a spiritual fight against sin). The ultimate purpose of Islam is the establishment by force of a worldwide Islamic state where Sharia law is enforced on all. To achieve this is the goal of Jihad. Islamic scholars identify a multitude of forms that Jihad can take:

There is the **Jihad of Words**, using oratory, in a war of nerves, to inspire their own side, and to undermine the morale of the enemy; the

A pastor and a deacon stand amidst the ashes of what was once a beautiful wooden church - destroyed by the Sudan Air Force.

Jihad of Deception to confuse the enemy; the **Jihad of the Sword** to kill the enemy, loot his possessions and take hostages for ransom; the **Jihad of Taxation** on non-Muslims and **Financial Reward** to provide incentives for converts to Islam; the **Jihad of Slavery** as a weapon to subjugate non-Muslims and as an economic incentive for the mujahadeens (or holy warriors); the **Jihad of Sharia Law** which degrades non-Muslims to a lower status, denied equal access to the law because their testimony is not valid against a Muslim; the **Jihad of Polygamy** which is designed to give Muslims a disproportionate numerical advantage through having up to 4 wives at a time; and the **Jihad of the Spirits**.

JIHAD AND "THE CRUSADES"

Inevitably when one deals with the contemporary problem of Islamic Jihad, someone will bring up the historical issue of the Christian Crusades. Of course, the word crusade does not appear in the Bible nor is it commanded in Scripture. However,

Jihad is both commanded in the Quran and practised by numerous Muslim groups and governments today.

To put the Crusades in their proper context, one needs to study the rapid expansion of Islam, by the sword, across North Africa, into Spain, throughout Asia Minor and into the Balkans. **The Islamic Jihad of the seventh to the tenth centuries wiped out more than half of the church**

A church in Nagarno Karabagh rocketed by Muslim Azerbaijanis.

worldwide. Prior to this, Christianity was the predominant religion of North Africa and the Middle East.

The Crusades of the Middle Ages were a reaction to the Islamic invasion of the Holy Lands (those places where our Lord was born, lived and ministered, was crucified and raised from the dead) and centuries of Islamic Jihad. The Saracens (as the Muslim invaders were called) had desecrated Christian places of worship and were severely persecuting Christians. Pilgrims were being prevented from visiting those sites sacred to their faith.

To this day many Muslims continue their *"holy war"* against Christians. Millions of Christians have been

Over 1,500,00 Christian Armenians were slaughtered by the Turks in 1915.

slaughtered through the centuries by Islamic militants – such as the over 1,500,000 Armenians murdered in Turkey in 1915.

JIHAD AND COLONIALISM

Others have sought to justify the Islamic practise of Jihad because they were "victims of colonialism"! This is quite a bizarre argument because the Muslim Arabs have been, perhaps, the most pervasive colonialists in history. Within the first century after Muhammad's death, the tribes of Arabia under the Caliphas had conquered Egypt, Libya, Tunisia, Algeria, Morocco, Spain, Portugal, Persia, parts of Byzantia and even parts of France.

Anti-American and Anti-Israel graffiti opposite a mosque in Cape Town's Malay Quarter.

The Muslim conquerors then enforced Arabic as the official medium of communication throughout North Africa and the Middle East. Only Turkey and Persia resisted this policy of Arabisation with any success. **Over 3,200 churches were destroyed or converted into mosques during the first century of Islamic Jihad alone.** The Muslim argument that Jihad was only waged in self-defence is therefore unconvincing. What were Arabians defending in Spain?

The Christian Blacks in Southern Sudan and the Nuba Mountains describe their conflict as a war of de-colonialisation from the Arab North.

JIHAD AND SLAVERY

After the fall of the Roman Empire in the 5th Century the practice of slavery declined throughout Europe. But the spread of Islam in the 7th Century led to a great revival of the institution of slavery, especially in Africa. Great merchant camel caravans travelled beyond the Sahara to the vast Savannah, which the Arabs called the Sudan (or *"the land of the Black People"*). These caravans brought back long lines of Black slaves for the Arab households and palaces on the Mediterranean. Male household servants were routinely castrated. Most babies born to Black slaves in the harems were drowned or killed at birth – to maintain Arab numerical superiority. One Arab writer in the 9th Century, justified this flourishing trade: *"the kings of the Blacks sell their own people without justification or in consequence of war."* (*History of Slavery*, Susanne Everett)

After crushing the slave trade in Sudan, General Charles Gordon was killed by the Mahdi's forces in Khartoum.

The horrors of the Islamic slave trade were well documented by explorers like David Livingstone, Samuel Baker, and the British Anti-Slavery Commissioner in East Africa, Sir John Kirk. These men set thousands of slaves free.

The Arab slave market in Zanzibar sold an average of 200 to 300 slaves every day, even as late as the 1870's. At one time, seven out of every eight Black people in Sudan were slaves.

The British Governor, General Charles Gordon, crushed the slave trade in Sudan, losing his life and being beheaded in the process. In recent years slavery has resurfaced in Sudan under the National Islamic Front government.

"...their works are works of iniquity, and the act of violence is in their hands. Their feet run to evil; and they make haste to shed innocent blood ... wasting and destruction are in their paths."
Isaiah 59: 6 –7

THE SUDAN CONNECTION

After the bombing attacks on the United States Embassies in Nairobi and Dar-es-Salaam on 7 August 1998 (which left over 260 dead and 5,000 injured) the US bombed targets in Sudan and Afghanistan, claiming that those governments supported Bin Laden's terrorist network. The US State Department's April 2001 *"Overview of State-sponsored Terrorism"* report states that *"Sudan continued to be used as a safe haven by members of various groups, including associates of Osama Bin Laden's Al-Qa'ida organisation, ... Egyptian Islamic Jihad, the Palestine Islamic Jihad and Hamas."*

"It was in Sudan that Bin Laden built the framework for his Al-Qa'ida terrorist

James Krama had his arm cut off by the Arabs after they burned his farm and looted his livestock.

group, which has branches around the world and thousands of young warriors willing to die in their Jihad against the United States and its allies. The Sudanese regime really gave birth to Osama Bin Laden, the terrorist." (National Post, Canada, 14/9/01).

The terrorist inclinations of the National Islamic Front government of Sudan, which hosted Bin Laden, is attested to by the savage way in which they continue to wage war against the Christian Blacks of Southern Sudan. *"In addition to the air attacks ... male villagers were killed in mass executions;*

women and children were nailed to trees with iron spikes ... soldiers slit the throats of children and killed male prisoners who had been interrogated by hammering nails into their foreheads. In Panyejie, last July, people had been crushed by tanks and strafed by helicopter gunships." ("Sudan – The Human Price of Oil" by Amnesty International, May 2000).

JIHAD AGAINST CHRISTIANS

There are at least 40 million Muslim youth in Madressas (Muslim religious schools) being taught to memorize the entire Quran and much of the Hadith. These schools have been described as *"breeding grounds for potential terrorists."*

There are 37,000 Madressas in Indonesia alone - the vast

Muslims in England publically call for the death of those who critise Islam.

majority of which are supportive of Bin Laden and vitriolically anti-American, anti-Christian, anti-Israel and anti-Jewish, glamourising the suicide bombers of the Intafada. These Madressas have been described as *"Jihad factories"*. The 1 million students in 10,000 madressas in Pakistan have been described as *"perfect jihad machines."* (*The Making of a Terrorist* by Jeffrey Goldberg, *Readers Digest* January 2002)

Fresh violence erupted in Africa's most populous nation, Nigeria, on 11 September 2001, as Muslim youths rushed onto the streets of Jos, shouting *"Allah Akbar"* and celebrating the news of the successful terror attacks against America. Soon, hundreds were dead in vicious street fighting between the Muslims and Christians. Many hundreds of churches have been destroyed and thousands of Christians killed by Muslim militants in Northern Nigeria. (*The Citizen*, 13/9/01)

Rev. Jeffrey Kayanga of the Episcopal Church of Sudan celebrates the Lord's Supper in the bomb-damaged Lui Cathedral on Resurrection Sunday.

In the Philippines and Indonesia, Christians continue to be beheaded and churches destroyed by Muslim terrorists. In Sudan, churches, hospitals, schools and mission stations have been subjected to repeated aerial bombardments by the National Islamic Front government of Sudan.

A CHRISTIAN RESPONSE

So what should be our response to the recent terror attacks and the ongoing Jihad against so many Christians worldwide?

Firstly, we need to recognise that this terrorism and anti-Christian persecution is originating from the least evangelised area of the world – the Middle East. The birthplace of the Church is now the most needy mission field on earth. **If we truly want to uproot the support bases of such terrorism and implode the regimes that persecute Christians, we need to get really serious about the Great Commission of our Lord Jesus Christ (Matthew 28:18 - 20).**

This will mean recognising that we are already in a spiritual world war. And **the only reason why the devil is so often winning**

One of the shipments of Bibles delivered to Southern Sudan by Frontline Fellowship.

is because the Church is so seldom fighting! We must not just retreat into our barracks to sing our battle songs – we must attack strongholds. We must not only talk about our spiritual weapons – we must use them. We must not only praise our Commanding Officer – we must obey Him. And the best form of defence is attack.

Now civil government has a ministry of **justice.** Under God they have a Biblical duty to protect their citizens, by bearing "the sword" and being "an agent of wrath to bring punishment on the wrongdoer." (Romans 13:4) That is their job.

Our duty in the Christian Church is to be a ministry of **grace.** We are to be *"a house of prayer for all nations"* (Mark 11:17); preaching *"repentance and forgiveness of sins … to all nations"* (Luke 24:47); making disciples of all nations and teaching obedience to all things that the Lord has commanded. (Matthew 28: 19-20).

We have a unique opportunity at this time of crisis to proclaim the Gospel of Christ effectively to Muslims all over the world. Instead of reacting with anger or malice, let us seek God's grace to reach out to our Muslim neighbours in Christian love.

This is the time when we can openly and politely discuss the differences between the Gospel and example of Christ and the teachings and actions of Muhammad. We can share our personal testimony and challenge Muslims to consider the claims of Christ. We can obtain and give Christian literature or Bibles to Muslims in our neighbourhood and we should invest in Christian radio programmes specifically designed to reach Muslims. Then we should wholeheartedly support missionary work in Muslim countries.

If Bin Laden can invest in translating the Quran into African languages and finance massive print runs of Islamic literature – then how much more should we as Christians invest in Bible translations and Christian literature!

By God's grace, Frontline Fellowship has already distributed over 300,000 Bibles and Christian books (much in Arabic) throughout Southern Sudan and the Nuba Mountains. We must do much more in future.

"The desert tribes will bow down to Him and His enemies will lick the dust … all kings will bow down to Him and all nations will serve Him." Psalm 72: 9-11

In addition, we must rediscover the imprecatory Psalms, the prayers for justice in the Bible. Many of the Psalms deal with the grief and trauma caused by treachery and violence. They channel our anguish and frustration in a positive way by appealing to God in prayer. Seeking justice from God is not only constructive and therapeutic, but of immense spiritual power. (See: War Psalms of the Prince of Peace by James Adams or Praying for Justice from FF).

"God will crush the heads of His enemies … of those who go on in their sins." Psalm 68:21

The Psalms are the prayer book of the Bible – I recommend that you pray through at least one Psalm each day. Make the Psalms the daily prayer of your heart. It will revive your prayer life. Terrorist attacks like those on 11 September 2001 should remind us that even the best security systems can fail to prevent such disasters. We need to rediscover God as our ultimate protection. The United States, in particular, should recognise its need for supernatural aid in defending its people and defeating terrorism. Elected representatives should incorporate respect and obedience to Almighty God into the constitution and public policy of the nation.

"Blessed is the nation whose God is the Lord." Psalm 33:12

A good place to begin would be to gather everyone for reading a chapter of Proverbs and praying a Psalm each day (either at the beginning of the day or at lunch time)in schools, army bases, businesses and government departments.

PREPARING FOR ETERNITY

We do not know when, or under what circumstances, our lives will come to an end. We do, however, know that when we die we will stand before Almighty God – our Creator and Eternal Judge – and we will have to give an account of our lives to Him. If you had died in those terror attacks of 11 September – where would you be now? And what would you be regretting?

"... it is appointed for men to die once, but after this the Judgement."   Hebrews 9: 27

We need to work out our priorities in the light of eternity. We need to invest our time, talents and treasure into those things which are going to last for eternity: the people of God, the Word of God and the Kingdom of God. These are what are ultimately important. You must be ready at all times for that which may happen at any time. **Are you ready?**

"Only one life, it will soon be past.
Only what's done for Christ will last."

An unexploded bomb which landed next to a church compound where we were ministering in Sudan.

Chapter 3

Resisting Sharia in Nigeria

Nigeria is a country of contrasts and conflict. Like Sudan, Nigeria has a Muslim north and a Christian south. However, unlike Sudan, in Nigeria it is the Christians who are the majority.

Just as Sudan is the largest country (2,503,890 square kilometres) in Africa, so Nigeria is the largest nation (120 million people in 490 ethnic groups). In fact, Nigeria has more Christians, and more Muslims, than any other country in Africa.

CHRISTIANS PERSECUTED

Christians have been severely persecuted in Nigeria's northern states. Literally hundreds of churches have been destroyed and thousands of Christians murdered in recent years.

One popular book, which is widely circulated amongst the Muslims in Nigeria, declares: ***"Priests in their churches ... should of course be killed without any exception*** ... *they should not build a church, nor leave one standing in an area controlled by the Muslims, if it is Muslim by force. Christians should not be allowed to hinder Muslims from being accommodated at their churches day or night. Gongs and bells should be hidden, no religious rites should be public. Christians should not display their religious convictions openly ... we are absolutely certain about declaring a person to be a kafir who belies or denies any of* *the foundations of the Shari'a or anything that is known by certainty to have been a deed by The Messenger ..."* The Sign of the Sword (1984) by Shaykh Abdalqadir Al-Murabit.

THE ISLAMIC AGENDA
Also well circulated in Nigeria is The Programme adopted by the **World Islamic Organisation** at a conference, in 1974, in Mecca:
   a. Muslim organisations should set up centres to resist Christian missionary activities.
   b. Islamic radio and TV stations should be established.
   c. All Christian activities, no matter the secular expression, should be stopped.
   d. Christian hospitals, orphanages, schools and universities should be taken over.
   e. Muslim organisations should set up Intelligence Centres about Christian activities.
   f. All Christian literature should be banned in Muslim countries.

1975, when General Murtala Muhammed overthrew General Yakubu Gowon, was the beginning of the implementation of this programme in Nigeria. Many streets bearing Christian names were changed to Muslim

names. Christian schools and hospitals were taken over by the state. Arabic inscriptions and emblems began to appear on Nigeria's currency notes and on emblems of the Nigerian Armed Forces.

At the **Islam in Africa Conference** in Abuja (1989) the Resolution issued at the conclusion of the conference declared their determination:

The Grand Mosque in the capital, Abuja, built with Mid-East oil money. The dome is gold plated.

"to show the whole world that Nigeria is truly an Islamic nation ... to support the establishment and application of the Shari'a ... **to ensure the appointment of only Muslims into strategic national and international posts of member nations.** *To* **eradicate in all its forms and ramifications all non-Muslim religions** *in member nations (such religions shall* **include Christianity** *...) to*

Between 1967 and 1970 Nigeria suffered a vicious civil war. The Federal forces, under Muslim control, slaughtered, or systematically starved, millions of Christian Igbos in the Biafran war.

ensure that only Muslims are elected *to political posts of all member nations. To ensure the declaration of Nigeria (the 24ᵗʰ African and 46ᵗʰ world member of the OIC) a Federal Islamic Sultanate ... to ensure the ultimate replacement of all Western forms of legal and judicial systems with the Shari'a in all member nations ... to write the history of Islam in Africa and of Muslims and their institutions from authentic Islamic viewpoint ... to propagate the knowledge of Islam throughout the continent ...* **to call on Muslims to review the syllabi in the various educational institutions with a view to bringing them into conformity with Islamic ideals, goals and principles** *and to serve the needs of their community ... to encourage the teaching of Arabic language, which is the language of the Qur'an as well as the lingua-franca of the continent and to* **strive for the restoration of the use of Arabic** *...to establish strong economic ties between African Islamic countries and other parts of the Muslim world in order to facilitate mutual assistance and co-operation ... based on Islamic principles."* Issued 28 November 1989 (1 Jumada al Awwal, 1410).

The Chairman of **the Bureau for Islamic Propagation**, Bashir Othman Tofa (a presidential candidate) declared: *"... these dangerous devils calling themselves Christians ... we Muslims cannot sacrifice our religion or our self-respect for any type of peaceful co-existence ... it is time to begin the offensive*

… let us begin by proclaiming Friday as our Sabbath … do away with the Christian Red Cross symbol … let us found our own Islamic Jihad of Nigeria to counteract the evil machinations of the Christian Association of Nigeria. Let us act right now!!!"

"ALL THE CHRISTIANS MUST BE SHOT"

The Muslim Brothers issued this statement which declared as their objective: ***"The establishment of the Shari'a of Allah and the destruction of Kafir from the face of the earth** … it is this Kafir system which gives these slaves (Christians)… It puts them on same level, it even raised the Christians higher than the Muslims … it is also necessary that we rise and destroy oppressors and the Kafir system … Ulamas should rise up and take the lead for the annihilation of Kafir … oh we are tired of Kafir system of government, Jewish Laws and decrees, and the rest acts of worship of Christianity on us … **all the Christians …. must be brought out to public and be shot**. From now on, Thursdays and Fridays must be work-free days … 'fight them until there remains no tumult (fitna) on the face of the earth and religion (way of life) becomes for Allah alone'. Quran"*

CHURCHES BURNED, CHRISTIANS MURDERED

During a ministry trip to Nigeria, I visited Lagos, Jos, Gboko and Abuja. I was shown numerous churches that had been damaged,

vandalised or burned down by Muslim mobs. And I received many heart-rending reports of Christians murdered by Muslims.

Many Christians bear the physical marks of bullet wounds, scars from machete wounds, cut off hands or feet, burns and deep slash marks on their necks and heads, inflicted by violent Muslim mobs.

One of the hundreds of churches that were burned down by Muslim mobs in Nigeria in recent years.

Twelve northern states in Nigeria have proclaimed Shari'a law. Literally hundreds of churches have been destroyed and thousands of believers murdered in Kaduna, Gombe, Sokoto, Kano and Bauchi. Central states, which are overwhelmingly Christian, have also borne the brunt of waves of Islamic Jihad. Thousands of Christians have been killed in Jos and Gboko, although the Christians in these areas have stood firm and resisted the Muslim offensives.

AFRICA'S LARGEST NATION

Nigeria is a huge country (923,768 Km²). The geography varies from the lush mangrove and tropical rainforests in the south to the savannah and grasslands in the north. Two huge rivers flow across the country - the Niger and the Benue.

Nigeria has over 120 million people in 490 ethnic groups. The three largest tribes are: the Hausa/Fulani, the Yoruba and Igbo.

Literacy is officially 64%. The official language of Nigeria is English, although Hausa is widely used in the northern states.

Nigeria is potentially rich in agricultural land and mineral resources, with large oil reserves. The enormous oil wealth of Nigeria has been squandered and embezzled by a series of corrupt rulers. Over 34% of the population live below the poverty line and unemployment is officially 28%.

MISSIONARY HERITAGE

Britain came to be involved in Nigeria primarily in order to crush the slave trade. Missionaries such as **Mary Slessor** and **Samuel Crowther** worked tirelessly to eradicate the slave trade, the killing of twins and other social evils. Samuel Crowther was a Yorubu who was captured by slave raiders and sold to Portuguese slave traders for transport across the Atlantic. Crowther was rescued by a British Naval squadron and received education in Sierra Leone and England. He was ordained by the Church of England and sent back to Yorubuland as a missionary. Crowther became the first African bishop of the Church of England.

TURBULENT TIMES

There was great optimism for the future when Nigeria received its independence from Britain in 1960. However, the post-independence history has been turbulent, with a vicious civil war, during which millions of Christian Igbos were starved or slaughtered by Federal forces. A succession of military coups, generally by Muslims, destroyed what was left of the post- independence optimism.

The sudden death of the brutal Muslim military dictator, Abacha, in 1998, brought General Olusegun Obasanjo, a committed Christian (converted while in prison in Jos), to the presidency. He has promised to eradicate corruption and bring about change, but there is great impatience and frustration at the pace and extent of the changes so far.

A concerted attempt by Muslim candidates to gain control in this first free election in the country's history ended with an overwhelming electoral victory for Obasanjo, and defeat for the Muslims.

SPECTACULAR CHURCH GROWTH

Amidst all the tensions, violence, coups and civil war, the churches in Nigeria have experienced spectacular growth. The Anglicans have grown from 900,000 in 1960 to over 12 million. SIM's work, which began at such great cost a century ago, has resulted in a dynamic church, ECWA (Evangelical Church of West Africa), with almost 5 million people. Evangelicals as a whole have grown from 2 million in 1960 to 28 million.

The Full Gospel Businessmen's Fellowship, with over 800 chapters, has had a significant impact on the commercial world.

Many Muslims have come to Christ despite death threats, discrimination and ostracism.

However, while there have been many successful evangelistic crusades, the widespread evangelism is seldom followed up with discipleship and Bible teaching. There has often been an over-emphasis on material prosperity, extravagance and sensationalism. There is a tremendous need for more leadership training and Bible colleges.

GREAT NEEDS, GREAT OPPORTUNITIES

Literature is highly sought after, but in very short supply. There are over 300 Christian bookshops in Nigeria, but stocks are severely limited by the price and lack of foreign exchange. The economic situation and poverty of most Christians place frustrating limitations on book availability and sales.

There is a great potential for Christian **radio** ministry in Nigeria. Over 85% of the population have a short-wave radio receiver and even more have access to FM. However, while both local and international radio broadcasts are used by Christians, the government has yet to allow an establishment of a Christian radio station inside Nigeria.

The church in Nigeria has become a significant **missionary sending** force. There are about 600 Nigerian missionaries serving in other lands, and thousands of Nigerian missionaries working within Nigeria, crossing linguistic and religious barriers to plant the Gospel in other communities.

There are over 160 **Bible colleges** and theological seminaries in Nigeria, however, most of these desperately need more quality Christian textbooks and qualified lecturers.

A new church in Abuja - the capital of Nigeria.

The government-controlled schools make provision for **religious education**. There are 15,000 Christian Religious Knowledge teachers in the state schools. They have great opportunities, but very limited resources.

Many hundreds of **Christian schools** have been launched by local churches, however, most of these use secular textbooks. There is a tremendous need for **Christian school textbooks** and Biblical Worldview training for Christian teachers.

In fact, it was the need for Christian textbooks and Leadership Training that led to my ministry trip to Nigeria when a Christian school gave me a Macedonian call: *"Come over and help us!"*.

THE FREE MARKET IN NIGERIA

My first impressions of Nigeria were of dozens of moneychangers with huge wads of notes swarming around me, offering to change Dollars, Pounds or Rands for Naira. Even late at night, the dark streets were lined with street vendors selling a bewildering array of goods and services by oil light. Hordes of 50 cc motorcycles and scooters, generally ridden by riders and passengers without helmets, weaved perilously fast between the fast-flowing battered vehicles and 3-wheeled taxis. The street vendors sold computers, photocopiers, laminators, satellite dishes, DVD and video machines and a wide range of other goods right on the sidewalk.

DRIVING ON THE OTHER SIDE

There were lots of army and police roadblocks, and many people dressed in Muslim robes. The heat was stifling and humid in Lagos, and I was soon pouring with sweat. Numerous mosques and churches were surrounded by street vendors.

Surprisingly, we were driving on the right-hand side of the road. Most of English-speaking Africa drive on the left. However, shortly after Independence, Nigeria decided to follow the practice of (French speaking) West Africa and the Arab nations by driving on the right.

Sometimes I was alarmed by the number of motorbikes driving towards us on the wrong side of the road – even on dual carriage ways – just to make their turn off quicker!

The dusty, crowded and pot-holed roads were incredible scenes of frantic speeding by a fascinating variety of vehicles. I was

Travel in Nigeria involves passing through many military checkpoints.

astonished to see even babies transported on motorbikes, sometimes just strapped to the mother's back by a blanket or towel. I saw one horrifying accident as a motorcyclist hit a young girl. I also saw lots of evidence of accidents along the side of the road: a petrol tanker rolled, huge 18-wheelers lying on their side, the cargo spilled over the roadside, pick-up trucks rolled, cars smashed and a burned-out truck on the main road.

MARKET PLACE AIRPORTS

Another first impression was the market place atmosphere in the airport terminals, with hordes of "helpers" giving advice as to which airline to use and offering all kinds of services.

Also surprising was how the check-in counters were barricaded behind solid bars, stretching from floor to ceiling. Behind these zoo-like bars, which would have been strong enough to keep an elephant out, were the check-in counters for a variety of airlines. I was told that one did not make prior bookings for internal flights, it was like boarding a bus.

Also surprising was when my host advised me to book on a 4pm flight, when it was already 4:15pm! *"No problem, it hasn't even started boarding yet!"* Sure enough, I made the 4pm flight, which departed at 5pm.

Security at the airport was also erratic. Sometimes the x-ray machines were faulty. On those occasions I was just waved through without even a hand-search of carry-on baggage.

Queuing for petrol in an oil exporting country.

CONTRASTS AND QUEUING IN AN OIL RICH COUNTRY

There was a sharp contrast between the palatial residences, off tree-lined streets, of government officials and squalid shacks of the over-crowded shantytowns surrounding the city centres.

I was surprised to find long petrol queues outside the fuel stations, especially as Nigeria is an oil-producing state – producing the 6th highest volume of oil in the world. Yet its citizens regularly have to queue up to obtain their oil, and there is a flourishing industry of entrepreneurs selling 5, 10 and 20 litre containers of petrol by the roadside – at greatly inflated prices of course (sometimes up to five times the fixed rate). But for those who want to avoid the queues or are in too much of a hurry to wait in line, there is generally no alternative.

DYNAMIC CHURCHES

Driving across Nigeria one is struck by the wide variety and vast quantity of churches. The names of the various congregations also give one an insight into the dynamic and innovative faith of the Nigerians: *"Deeper-life Bible Church", "Evangelical Church of West Africa", "Full Gospel Church", "Victory Faith Church", "Grace and Truth Tabernacle", "The Triumphant Church", "Living Faith Winners Chapel", "Throne Voice of Power", "Redeemed*

People", "Watchmen Catholic Charismatic Renewal Movement", "Solid Rock Fellowship", "Full Anointed Gospel Power Church", "Power Revival Ministries" and so many others.

In every community I visited, I saw numerous church buildings under construction.

Each church I visited was well organised, with the presentations being audio & video taped. The audio & video tapes were available, on sale, before the end of the day.

There was a real intensity in the times of prayer and worship. Services were normally long. One meeting in Gboko went on for six hours without a break. I found the churches in Nigeria to have strong evangelistic concern and missionary vision.

SUPPORTING TYRANTS

There was also a growing social concern, with many expressing their frustration and disappointment that their government was not standing with the suffering people of Zimbabwe, but rather supporting the dictator, Mugabe.

It was remembered that previous Nigerian governments had supported other tyrants such as Idi Amin who, while Chairman of the Organisation of African Unity, was massacring Christians in his country. It was remembered that even though only 6% of the population of Uganda were Muslims, Idi Amin declared Islam the official religion of Uganda. Many hundreds of thousands of Christians were murdered under Idi Amin's brutal regime – yet most African leaders remained silent about the Ugandan Holocaust.

> *"Cease to do evil; Learn to do good; seek justice, rebuke the oppressor; defend the fatherless, plead for the widow."*
> Isaiah 1:16-17

Similarly, during Mengistu's *Red Terror* in Ethiopia, Samora Machel's persecution of the Church in Mozambique and Augestino Neto's reign of terror in Angola, these tyrants were well received and supported throughout Africa, including in Nigeria.

The Christians I spoke to were disturbed about the silence on Mugabe's racism and lawlessness. *"This is a disgrace and a disaster for Africa. While Mugabe is destroying agriculture and ruining the economy, he is also killing tourism and chasing away investment – not only for Zimbabwe but for all Africa."*

Others mentioned their disappointment at US president Bill Clinton who during his visit to Nigeria in August 2000 remained silent on the brutal oppression and persecution of Christians in the North of the country. They felt betrayed by his silence on Nigeria's most acute human rights problem.

"Hate evil, love good; establish justice in the gate."

Amos 5:15

SLAUGHTER UNDER SHARI'A

Of greatest concern to the Nigerian Christians that I had fellowship with was the threat of Shari'a Law from the Muslims.

In Jos, on 7th September 2001, during Friday afternoon prayers, a Muslim mob beat a pregnant Christian woman to death. They claimed

A pastor stands in the ashes of a church building in Jos destroyed by Muslim mobs in January 2010.

The Muslim candidate for the first-ever presidential elections, Buhari, was soundly defeated.

that she had walked past them while they were bowed in prayer, outside the Mosque. In rage, they got up from their prayer mats and savagely beat her, killing both the woman and her pre-born child.

Not satisfied with this innocent blood, the Muslims then went on the rampage down the main street in Jos, burning churches, shops and homes. Many hundreds of Christians were beaten, shot or hacked to death by these Muslim mobs.

RESISTANCE IN JOS

The next day, the Christians rallied and stood firm together, resisting the Islamic attacks.

> *"Do not be afraid of them. Remember the Lord, great and awesome, and fight for your brethren, your sons, your daughters, your wives and your houses."* Nehemiah 4:14

More Christians poured in from the surrounding villages, some wearing traditional warrior regalia and brandishing spears, axes and machetes. Vicious hand-to-hand fighting took place on the streets, and many firearms were captured from the Muslims. Some Christians counterattacked and by the end of the week, over 6,000 people had been killed.

The Gospel was first established among the Tiv people by South African Reformed missionaries in 1903. For the last 100 years the Tiv have resisted Islam.

The Muslims were completely defeated and many were fleeing north. Throughout this conflict the police and army were unseen – barricaded in their barracks.

Upon investigation, it was revealed that the Muslim community had been planning this attack for many months, stockpiling weapons and ammunition. They were looking for a pretext to trigger their assault. The Christian woman walking past the Mosque was seized as an ideal opportunity for them to initiate their attack. **What they had not expected was such fierce resistance from the Christians.** Many Muslims said that they had never expected the Christians to fight back.

The Christians in Jos related to me numerous examples of the Lord's protection in answer to prayer. A truck carrying weapons for Muslims crashed outside Jos, spilling and revealing a weapons cache. There have been numerous other Muslim plots which have been exposed.

CHRISTIAN COURAGE IN GBOKO

In Gboko, the Tiv people related to me testimonies of how the Muslim Hausa and Fulani people attacked their homes and churches, burning down entire communities. When the Federal forces were sent in to restore order, they burned even more farms and houses. The units sent were predominantly Muslim and under Muslim control, so rather than restoring order, they joined in the assaults against the Christians, massacring whole villages. **In Vaase, 1,200 civilians were killed** by these Muslim Federal forces. In Taraba state, up to **100 churches were destroyed by Muslim mobs.** The long-suffering Tiv people also rose up and resisted, fighting back. All this happened in August and September 2002.

Over 80% of the schools in Tivland are owned by the churches. However, none had a Christian curriculum. There is a desperate need for Christian textbooks.

BETWEEN CROSS AND CRESCENT

Despite the stresses of continual Islamic pressure and persecution, the mature and dynamic Church in Nigeria is standing firm and reaching out vigorously to its Muslim neighbours.

Christians in Lagos, Nigeria, participating in a Frontline Fellowship Great Commission Conference.

Nigerian Christians at a Muslim Evangelism Workshop intercede for their Muslim neighbours.

The conflict between the Cross and the Crescent in Nigeria is intensifying. Muslim nations are pouring in vast millions to fund the construction of Mosques, Madressas and Muslim schools, and to promote Shari'a Law throughout Nigeria.

The Christians are responding by establishing more churches and Christian schools and through literature and radio ministry. They need our encouragement, prayers and support. We have the opportunity in Nigeria not only to help the Christians stand firm and resist the southern encroachments of Islam, but also to roll back the Islamic offensive, winning their enemies to Christ.

"The harvest is plentiful, but the workers are few. Ask the Lord of the Harvest therefore to send out workers into His harvest field." Matthew 9:37

Chapter 4

Jihad - Islamic Holy War

he relentless and often vicious persecution by Muslims against Christians is seldom recognised or understood. Many assume that the concept of Jihad, or Holy War, espoused by Muslim leaders like the Ayatollah Khomeini, was an aberration not truly representative of Islam:

*"We shall export our revolution, to the whole world. Until the cry **'Allah Akbar'** resounds over the whole world. There will be struggle. There will be Jihad... Islam is the religion of militant individuals ... Islam will be victorious in all the countries of the world, and Islam and the teachings of the Quran will prevail all over the world ... This is the duty that all Muslims must fulfill. . ."* These were the often repeated public pronouncements of the Ayatollah Khomeini after the revolution in Iran in 1979 (Quoted from *"The Blood of the Moon"* by George Grant).

Lt. Gen. Al Bashir and Dr. Al Turabi.

Christians in Southern Sudan have resisted Islamic Jihad for generations.

Nor was the Ayatollah alone in such militant threats. Abdul Aziz Ibn Saud declared:

"We shall never call for or accept a negotiated peace. We shall only accept war – Jihad – the holy war. We have resolved to drench the lands of Palestine and Arabia with the blood of the infidels or to accept Martyrdom for the glory of Allah."

The President of Sudan, Lt. Gen. Al Bashir often speaks of *Jihad.* At the 40th anniversary of Sudan's independence, Al Bashir celebrated the spirit of *Jihad* which was engulfing the people of Sudan. The head of Sudan's ruling party, the *National Islamic Front* (NIF), Dr. Al Turabi, has often declared his goal of an Islamic empire controlling (initially) the horn of Africa (Eritrea, Ethiopia, Somalia, Kenya, Uganda and Sudan). This he calls the Grand Islamic Project.

At a two week conference of Muslim leaders from 80 countries, hosted by Muammar Gaddafi in Tripoli, Libya (October 1995), strategies to transform Africa into an Islamic continent were discussed. Participants openly admitted that their goals were to make Arabic the primary language of the continent and Islam the official religion. One SA member of parliament, Farouk Cassim declared: *"It will probably be the biggest revolution to sweep Africa."* Head of the Islamic Propagation Centre International (IPCI), Yousuf Deedat, announced afterwards that South Africa was high on the agenda of the Islamic offensive. *"We are going to turn South Africa into a Muslim state. We have the money to do it,"* he said (Sunday Times 22/10/95). At present less than 2 percent of South Africans are Muslims.

What few Westerners understand, however, is that those Muslim leaders who call for the overthrow of all governments and the establishment of an Islamic superstate controlling all aspects of life for every person on earth are not extremists on the fringe of Islam. Actually, *Jihad* (the subjugation and forcible conversion of all people to Islam and world domination) are central tenets of Islam. *Jihad* is ranked by many Muslims as the sixth pillar of Islam.

Jihad was so important to Muhammad that he declared it to be the second most important deed in Islam.

"Allah's apostle was asked, 'What is the best deed?' He replied, 'To believe in Allah and his Apostle.' The questioner then asked, 'What is the next (in goodness)?' He replied, 'To participate in Jihad (religious fighting) in Allah's cause.'" – The Hadith, Al Bukhari, Vol. 1 no 25.

Muslims in fact divide the world into two sectors: _Dar-al-Islam_ (the House of Islam) and _Dar-al-Harb_ (The House of War). The only countries considered to be at peace are those where Islamic law (the _Sharia_) is enforced. Islam does not recognize the right of any other religion or worldview to exist.

Islam in Arabic means submission, surrender or subjugation. A *Muslim* is one who submits. The Arabic word for peace is *Salam*. *Islam* is the active form of *Salam*. Muslims see

Muslims have desecrated Christian graveyards in Southern Sudan.

themselves as a *"peace making force"* using argument, intrigue, commerce, threats, terrorism, warfare and every other means possible to secure Islam as the only religion worldwide.

Muslims are not permitted to make peace with a non-Muslim country until its inhabitants surrender to Islam. They can agree to a cease fire for a period of time – but never to peace with non-Muslims.

The Quran teaches that Muslims are superior to others: *"Ye (Muslims) are the best of peoples evolved for mankind . . ."* Surah 3:110.

Muslims are forbidden to befriend Jews or Christians: *"O ye who believe! Take not the Jews and the Christians for your friends and protectors. They are but friends and protectors to each other. And he amongst you that turns to them (for friendship) is one of them . . ."* Surah 5:54.

Islam instructs its adherents to fight until their opponents submit. Christians and Jews may be spared if they pay *"Jizya"* – a penalty tax – with willing submission: *"Fight those who believe not in God nor the last day . . . Nor acknowledge the religion of truth, (even if they are) of the people of the Book, until they pay Jizya (tribute taxes) with willing submission, and feel themselves subdued."* Surah 9:29

"Fight and slay the pagans wherever ye find them and seize them, beleaguer them, and lie in wait (ambush) for them in every stratagem (of war); but if they repent and establish regular prayers and practise regular charity, then open the way for them." Surah 9:5 (also 2:193).

For those who resist Islam – execution or mutilation is decreed: *"The punishment of those who wage war against Allah and His apostle, and strive with might and main for mischief through the land is: execution or crucifixion, or the cutting off of the hands and feet from opposite sides or exile from the land . . ."* Surah 5:36.

The **Hadith** which is a record of the words and deeds of Muhammad is also viewed by Muslims as inspired. Next to the Quran, it is the most important source of Islamic Law. Its teachings are regarded as binding on all Muslims.

The Hadith teaches that apostasy is punishable by death: *"Whoever changes his Islamic religion, kill him."* Vol. 9:57.

A Muslim may not be punished for killing a non-Muslim: *"No Muslim should be killed for killing a kafir (infidel)."* Vol 9:50

Those who die in holy war are guaranteed to go to Heaven. *"The person who participates in Jihad (Holy battles) in Allah's cause and nothing compels him to do so except belief in Allah and His apostle,*

Graffiti in Cape Town Malay Quarter - a Jihad of words.

will be recompensed by Allah either with a reward or booty (if he survives) or will be admitted to paradise (if he is killed)." Vol 1:35

It may be hard for Christians to understand the concept of such a militant religion, but the primary aim of Islam is not spiritual but political. The ultimate purpose of Islam is the establishment by force of a worldwide Islamic state where *Sharia* law is enforced on all.

To achieve this is the goal of *Jihad*. Islamic scholars identify a multitude of forms that Jihad can take.

1. There is **the Jihad of Words.** Muhammad was a brilliant and gifted orator silencing his enemies in a war of words. In Arab culture it was customary for feuding tribes to select a poet to mock and provoke the opposing forces with spontaneous verses of cursing. These linguistic warriors engaged in verbal combat sought to inspire their own side with a sense of superiority and strength whilst undermining the morale of the enemy. This war of words, which Muslim leaders such as Gaddaffi, Saddam Hussein and Yassir Arafat have engaged in, is actually a war of nerves.

2. There is **the Jihad of Deception.** When Muslims are small in number they can follow the example of Muhammad's 83 followers who fled from persecution in Mecca to Abyssinia (present day Ethiopia). There the Christian *Negus* (king) offered them refuge. When the Meccans demanded their return as slaves, the Muslim exiles declared that Islam was merely a variation of Christianity. The Muslims selectively recited those passages of the Quran that agreed with the Bible such as the virgin birth and miracles of Jesus and His ascension to Heaven and ultimate return. They remained silent on the unbridgeable differences (such as the denial of the Trinity and the atonement) between the Quran and the Bible. As a result the Christian Abyssinians protected the Muslims from the Meccans. In this way, when it was most vulnerable, Islam grew and developed in a Christian environment. (If we only demonstrate our Christian love without proclaiming the truth of the Gospel we could be strengthening anti-Christian forces). Muhammad also compromised with the Meccan merchants during a particularly intense time of persecution. Formerly he had fearlessly condemned polytheism. Then, under pressure, he accepted the Meccan belief that Allah had a wife, *Al-lat,* and two daughters, *Al Uzzo* and *Manat* (Surah 53:20-23). Later Muhammad repudiated these so called *Satanic Verses* and claimed that all previous prophets had been tempted by demonic influence.

Muslims in England call for beheadings of those who insult Islam and threaten Europe with its own 9-11.

Arab slave raiders attack a village in East Africa, 1880.

3. There is **the Jihad of the Sword.** After fleeing to Medina *(the HIJRA)* in AD622, Muhammad started to summon his followers to attack and plunder the caravans of Mecca. His followers initially resisted these calls until Muhammad presented a series of *"revelations"* commanding *Jihad* (holy war) and permitting looting *("Whoever has killed an enemy and has proof of that, will possess his spoils"* – The Hadith, Vol. 4 no. 370). Where the booty was not large enough, Muhammad held captives as hostages until their families paid a high ransom for their release. Hostage taking has been a common practice in Islam to this day. Those who participate in *Jihad* are granted a blanket absolution (Surah 8:17) and guaranteed to go straight to Paradise (Heaven) if killed. **Anyone who is not a Muslim is assumed to be rejecting Islam. Resisting Islam equates to attacking Islam and therefore inviting Jihad! Hence any war against any non-Muslim can be condoned as** *"defensive"* **by such Islamic** *"reasoning".*

4. There is **the Jihad of Taxation and Financial Reward.** Those who refuse to submit to Islam are forced to pay a special extortionary tax for non-Muslims *(Jizya)*. Those who convert to Islam are offered financial rewards or scholarships. *Jizya* helps finance *Jihad*.

5. There is **the Jihad of Slavery.** Those Muslims who engage in *Jihad* not only can seize property, extort ransoms and demand taxes, but also capture slaves. The only places in the world today where slavery is still practised are in some Muslim countries. In Sudan, the Islamic government uses slavery as an incentive to encourage Arab Northerners to attack the Christian Blacks in the South and as a weapon of terror to destabilise non Muslims. According to the *Sharia*, Muslims are allowed to enslave, own and sell human beings.

6. There is **the Jihad of *Sharia* law.** Non-Muslims are degraded to a lower class status and are denied equal access to the law because their testimony is not valid against a Muslim. This even applies to

When the Mahdi captured Khartoum, in 1885, he put all the inhabitants of the city to death.

murder *("No Muslim should be killed for killing an infidel").* The death penalty is applied to anyone who renounces Islam and converts to another religion. When the wealthy Bedouins of Arabia professed faith in Allah to escape attack, Muhammad did not accept their confession. *("The desert Arabs say 'We believe'. Say, 'Ye have no faith; but ye (only) say 'We have submitted.'"* Surah 49:14) Islam does not place much value on personal faith, but demands surrender to the political rule of the *Sharia.* It is significant that the calendar of Islam does not begin with the birth of Muhammad, nor the onset of his supposed *"revelation"*, nor the assembling of the first Muslim community, nor the flight of Muslim refugees to Abyssinia. The 12 years of persecution in Mecca were not considered the start of their new religion. The Muslim calendar only begins when Islam became a political state in Medina.

7. There is **the Jihad of Polygamy.** The devastating defeat of the Muslim forces by the Meccans in the battle of Uhud (AD625) led to what could be considered one of Islam's greatest victories. So many of his men were killed that Muhammad permitted his men to take up to 4 wives (Surah 4:3, 4). With the advent of Western medicine, infant mortality has plummeted. And the Muslim birthrate has skyrocketed. Muslims are increasing in number twice as fast as other religions. This is due to birth control and abortion in Western lands and polygamy in Muslim lands. Muslims are not increasing much by missionary outreaches, but by having many children. Polygamy has become one of Islam's most effective weapons for Holy War, providing Islam with a disproportionate numerical advantage.

8. There is **the Jihad of the spirits.** According to the Quran, Muslims are not only men and women but also spirits who fight for the spread of Islam (Surah 46:29-33 and 72:1-15). A Muslim is to fight on Muhammad's behalf both in his life and after his death (Hadith Vol. 1 chapter 43).

Millions of Europeans and Africans were enslaved by Muslims in the Middle East.

Clearly Islam is a religion of force which denies basic freedom. It may not be politically correct to say so, but pretending that the Quran is a pacifist document and that Islam has a consistent track record of peace and tolerance is either foolish or deceitful. We need to have the courage and integrity to describe an intolerant religion of violence and oppression as it is. No Muslim has the freedom even to change or leave his religion. **The huge block of over one billion Muslims presents the greatest political and military threat to the free world and the greatest missionary challenge to the Christian Church. Muslim states are the most severe persecutors of Christians, and Muslim terrorist groups are the most vicious hijackers, kidnappers, bombers and assassins. Islam is a challenge that we cannot ignore.**

How we choose to respond, in prayer, publications, projects and persistent vigilance will determine much of the course of history in the 21st Century.

Chapter 5

Islam According to The Reformers

In expounding Daniel 9, Martin Luther noted that among others, the prophet Daniel was talking about the Muslim Turks, who at that time were invading Europe: *"In the latter part of their reign, when rebels have become completely wicked, a stern-faced king, a master of intrigue will arise. He will become very strong, but not by his own power. He will cause astounding devastation ... He will cause deceit to prosper and he will consider himself superior. When they feel secure, he will destroy many and take his stand against the Prince of princes. Yet he will be destroyed, but not by human power."* Daniel 8:23 – 25

Martin Luther launched the Protestant Reformation.

Luther wrote that the *"two regimes, that of the Pope and that of the Turk, are ... antichrist."*

John Calvin in a sermon on Deuteronomy 18:15 maintained that Muhammad was one of *"the two horns of antichrist."*

In his commentaries on Daniel (7: 7 – 18), Calvin put forward the theory that the Muslim Turks were the little horn that sprang up from the beast. As the Turks had conquered much of the old Roman Empire, much of the prophecies concerning Rome could apply to the Muslim world. Islam was one of the two legs of the later Roman Empire described in Daniel 2.

Commenting on Daniel 11:37, Calvin wrote that Muhammad *"allowed to men the brutal liberty of chastising their wives and thus he corrupted that conjugal love and fidelity which binds the husband to the wife ... Mohamet allowed full scope to various lusts – by permitting a man to have a number of wives ... Mohamet invented a new form of religion."* (Commentaries on the Book of the Prophet Daniel – John Calvin).

Luther noted that Christ warned about false prophets coming from the desert (Matthew 24: 24 – 26) and this certainly included Muhammad.

Commenting on 2 Thessalonians 2: 3 – 12, Calvin wrote that ... *"the sect of Mohammad was like a raging overflow, which in its violence tore away about half of the church."*

In his commentary on 1 John 2: 18 – 23, Calvin states that the Turks *"have a mere idol in place of God."*

Luther observed from 1 John 2: 18 – 22 and 4: 1 – 3, *"Who is the liar? It is the man who denies that Jesus is the Christ. Such a man is the antichrist – he denies the Father and the Son."* 1 John 2: 22, that the Mohammadans deny both the Fatherhood of God and the Deity of Christ – hence they are liars. They testify against the truth of God's Word.

On 1 John 4: 3 – 6: *"but every spirit that does not acknowledge Jesus, is not from God. This is the spirit of the antichrist ... this is how we recognise the spirit of truth and the spirit of falsehood"*, Calvin noted that *"Mohammad too asserts that he has drawn his dreams only from Heaven ... False spirits claim the Name of God."*

Luther observed that the Muslim Turks want *"to eradicate the Christians."*

The 1637 Calvinist Dordt Bible in Dutch, comments on Revelation 16:12 that the Muslim nations of the East would still unite with one another in a Pan-Islamic Jihad against the West.

The 1643 Westminster Assembly's "Larger Catechism" calls on Christians to ... *"pray, that the kingdom of sin and Satan may be destroyed, that the Gospel propagated throughout the world ..."* "The Directory for the Public Worship of God" instructs congregations to *"pray for the propagation of the Gospel and Kingdom of Christ to all nations, for the conversion of the Jews, the fullness of the Gentiles, the fall of antichrist, and the deliverance of the distressed Churches abroad from the tyranny of the anti Christian faction, and from the cruel oppression and blasphemies of the Turk."*

John Calvin - the Reformer of Geneva.

Commenting on Rev. 9: 1 – 11, the Dutch Dordt Bible of 1637 suggests that Muhammad is *"Apollyon"* (which is Greek for the Hebrew word *"Abaddon"* which means destroyer) and the army of locusts and scorpions are the Arab and Saracen armies which wage *Jihad* in Muhammad's name.

In his Institutes (Book 2, chapter 6:4), Calvin writes: *"So today the Turks, although they proclaim at the top of their lungs that the Creator of Heaven and earth is God, still, while repudiating Christ, substitute an idol in the place of the true God."*

Jonathan Edwards, the first President of Princeton University, wrote in his "A History of the Work of Redemption": *"The two great works of the devil which he ... wrought against the Kingdom of Christ are ... his Anti-Christian*

Jonathan Edwards who preached "Sinners in the Hands of an angry God".

(Romish or Papal) and Mohametan (Muslim or Islamic) kingdoms ... which have been, and still are, two kingdoms of great extent and strength. Both together swallow ... up the Ancient Roman Empire; the (Papal) kingdom of Antichrist swallowing up the Western Empire, and Satan's Mohametan kingdom the Eastern Empire ... In the Book of Revelation (chapters 16 – 20) ... it is in the destruction of these that the glorious victory of Christ at the introduction of the glorious times of the Church, will mainly consist..."

In a sermon on 2 Timothy 1:3, Calvin explained: *"The Turks at this day, can allege and say for themselves: 'We serve God from our ancestors!' ... It is a good while ago since Mahomet gave them the cup of his devilish dreams to drink, and they got drunk with them. It is about a thousand years since those cursed hellhounds were made drunk with their follies ... Let us be wise and discreet! ... For otherwise, we shall be like the Turks and Heathen!"* (Sermons on Timothy and Titus – John Calvin).

Calvin pointed out that the reign of antichrist will be destroyed by the Word of God (2 Thessalonians 2:8). *"Paul does not think that Christ will accomplish this in a single moment ... Christ will scatter the darkness in which antichrist will reign, by the rays which He will emit before His coming – just as the sun, before becoming visible to us, chases away the darkness of the night with its bright light.*

"This victory of the Word will therefore be seen in the World. For 'the Breath (or Spirit) of His Mouth' means simply His Word ... as in Isaiah 11:4, the passage to which Paul appears to be alluding ... It is a notable commendation of true and sound doctrine that it is represented as being sufficient to put an end to all ungodliness,

and as destined at all times to be victorious over all devices of Satan. It is also a commendation when ... a little further on ... the preaching of this doctrine, is referred to as Christ's 'coming' to us." (Commentary on Second Thessalonians - John Calvin).

"The Kingdoms of this world have become the Kingdom of our Lord and of His Christ, and He shall reign forever and ever." Revelation 11:15

"All nations will come and worship before You ..." Revelation 15:4

AD 732 Charles Martel, King of the Franks, ordered every man able to bear arms to repulse the Muslim invaders. The Christian army met the Arab cavalry on the plains of Tours. They stood firm and broke the six furious charges of the Muslims. The next day the Muslim invaders fled from France to back behind the Pyrenees.

"The desert tribes will bow before Him and His enemies will lick the dust ... All kings will bow down to Him and all nations will serve Him." Psalm 72:9-11

Reformer Martin Luther taught that Islam is antichrist and would be destroyed - "but not by human hands".

Chapter 6

The Sources of Islam

One out of every six people in the world is a Muslim. 1,200 million people from the Philippines to the Atlantic coast of the Sahara Desert live under the control of Islam.

Islam is a missionary religion, full of religious zeal and aggressive energy. Every year thousands of Muslim missionaries graduate from the Universities of Cairo, Tripoli and Tehran and are sent out to propagate Islam. Yet even as the Muslim government of Afghanistan bulldozed the only Protestant church building in the country, a splendid R7.5 million mosque was opened in London. Despite Algeria expelling a one-hundred-year-old Christian missionary society, a Muslim missionary society began work in Canada. Even though missionary work, or conversion to Christianity, is illegal in Saudi Arabia, Muslim missionaries from that country are working in Britain to convert committed Christians to Islam.[2]

Even while Islam is being propagated in Europe and America, the heads of 37 Muslim countries resolved to expel all Christian missionaries from their lands.[3] Islam has been the largest and most vicious opponent and persecutor of the Church throughout the centuries.

By the 10th Century, Muslims had annihilated 50% of all the Christians in the world of that time. Today, repression of Christians in Muslim lands continues.

Islam is the greatest challenge to the whole Christian Church today. They claim to worship God in a better way than Jews or Christians. They believe they adhere to a more strict monotheistic faith. They say that Christians are not living true to the revealed Will of God. They seek to convert Christians to Islam.

Muslims make up the largest group of unreached people in the world today. Islam is the great final frontier for Christian missions. They appear an impenetrable fortress that Christian missionaries must storm and breach in order to fulfill Christ's command to:

> *"Go throughout the whole world and preach the Gospel to all mankind."*   Mark 16:15

> *"Go, then, to all peoples everywhere and make them My disciples."*   Matthew 28:19

The question that Christians must face is this: Where did Islam come from – from God, from man or from the devil? To understand and answer the challenge of Islam, we must investigate its sources. We can only determine its true nature by uncovering its roots.

THE AUTHORITY OF ISLAM

The foundation of Islam is a book, about the same length as the New Testament, written (or recited) in the 7th Century A.D. by Muhammad. This is what Muslims claim:

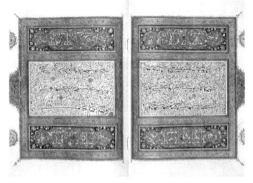

Open Quran.

> *"The Quran was revealed to the Holy Prophet Muhammad (Peace be on Him) who was born in Mecca, Arabia, in the year 571 after Jesus. The revelations*

were sent by Allah (God), brought by the Archangel Gabriel and were given, taught and explained to the Holy Prophet Muhammad (PBOH) . . . The Holy Prophet Muhammad continued to receive these revelations for 23 years."[4]

"In the world today the Holy Quran is the ONLY REVEALED BOOK of Allah which has remained spotlessly pure and UNCHANGED from the date of its revelation fourteen hundred years ago. Each WORD as found in the Quran today is EXACTLY the same today as when it was first revealed by Allah to the Holy Prophet Muhammad (PBOH). For fourteen centuries no man or group of men has succeeded in changing or altering a single word or even a dot of the Holy Quran."[5]

The Quran claims that it could not possibly have been produced by anyone but God Himself.

"Say: Verily, though mankind and Jinn (evil spirits) should assemble to produce the like of this Quran, they could not produce the like thereof though they were helpers one of another." Surah 17:88

"And this Quran is not such as could ever be invented in despite of Allah." Surah 10:37

Islam holds the Quran as its authority and foundation. It maintains that the Quran is of divine origin and furthermore that it is impossible that it could have been invented or produced by mankind.

Now, it follows that if we can show that significant parts of the Quran were derived from human systems or existing sources available in Muhammad's time, then the great claims of Islam collapse.

It has been alleged that Islam:

". . . is simply Talmudic Judaism adapted to Arabia, plus the Apostleship of Jesus and Muhammad . . . The sources (according to Mr Rodwell, a Quran translator) whence Muhammad derived the materials of his Quran are, over and above the more poetical parts, which are his own creation, the legends of his time and country, Jewish traditions based upon the Talmud, and the Christian traditions of Arabia and of Syria."[6]

ARABIAN SOURCES OF THE QURAN
Allah

The Arabian people worshipped at a small temple called the Ka'aba and had a deity with poorly defined characteristics, who was called

Muslim pilgrims taking part in the Hajj.

The Ka'aba in Mecca.

simply *"the god"*, which in Arabic is *"Allah"*. At that time there was a general idea among Arabs that there was only one supreme being. Some Arabs were even beginning to identify the God of the Jews and Christians with Allah, the god of the Ka'aba.[7]

The Ka'aba and Hajj

The Ka'aba, which is also called the Holy Masjid, was described as a shrine of worship in Mecca as early as 60 B.C. by Deodorus Sicobus.[9] Men from all over Arabia came to the Ka'aba to worship[10]; pilgrimages were well known and practised before Muhammad instituted the Hajj as the fifth pillar of faith. Muslims claim that the Ka'aba was built by Abraham, although the Bible does not teach this and Abraham never even visited Mecca.

Salat

The practice of ritual prayer (salat) can be traced to the now extinct tribe of the Sabaeans who lived in the Arabian Peninsula and observed seven daily prayers at set times. The Sabaeans also prayed for the dead, a custom that is still practised by Muslims today.[11]

Ramadan

The Muslim practice of fasting from sunrise to sundown every day during the holy month of Ramadan can also be traced back to the Sabaeans. They fasted 30 days every year and celebrated the Eid sacrifice. The fast was prolonged by one day, should the new moon not be clearly visible on Eid. Again this practice was incorporated into the new religion of Islam.[12] In the Jewish Mishna Berkhoth (Talmud), it was said that fasting should begin and end at the time when one could distinguish between a white and black thread. This custom, too, has been incorporated into Islamic traditions.[13]

JEWISH SOURCES OF THE QURAN

In the Arabian Peninsula there were many Jewish communities living in the *diaspora*, which had resulted from the destruction of Jerusalem in 70 A.D. There was a synagogue in Medina and Muhammad had much contact with the Jews. These Arabian Jews seem to have been more guided by legends and Talmudic writings rather than by the Torah.

Cain and Abel

The way the story of Cain and Abel is related in Surah 5:30-35 shows that it was copied from the Targum of Jonathan-ben-Uzziah, the Targum of Jerusalem and Pirkê Rabbi Eleazar.[14]

Abraham

Muhammad clearly did not learn of Abraham from Genesis but rather from Jewish legends. The stories of Abraham being saved from Nimrod's fire, and of Abraham's father getting him to sell idols he had made, are copied from the Midrash Rabbâh. At any rate, Nimrod lived many generations before Abraham, so the story is not historical.[15]

The Visit of the Queen of Sheba

In Surah 27 the story of the visit of the Queen of Sheba is related. Although the Quran reports this to be from the Bible, it differs radically from 1 Kings 10:1-13 and 2 Chronicles 9:1-12. In fact, the Quranic account is from 11 Targum of the Talmudic book of Esther.[16] Perhaps Muhammad, hearing the story from his Jewish contacts, assumed that it was derived from the Torah.

Hârût and Mârût

The two angels named in Surah 2:102, Hârût and Mârût, were idols worshipped in Armenia. Their story was related in the Talmud (Midrash Yalzut, chapter 44).[17]

Satan's Refusal to Worship Adam

The legend of satan refusing to worship Adam, as reported in Surah 2:34, can also be traced back to the Jewish Talmud.[18]

Seven Heavens and Seven Hells

This story, as reported in Surah 15:44 and 17:44, is derived from the tradition called Hagigah and Zuhal.[19]

Qibla

This practice of facing in a set direction when praying was a Jewish practice. The Quran first commanded Muslims to pray towards Jerusalem, but when the Jews fell into disfavour with Muhammad, he changed the direction to Mecca (Surah 2:142).[20]

CHRISTIAN SOURCES OF ISLAM

Muhammad also had much contact with Christians of some type or another.

"Monophysite Christianity was at that time widely spread in the Arab kingdom of Ghassan; the Byzantine Church was represented by hermits dotted about the Hijaz with whom he may well have come into contact; the Nestorians were established at Al Hira and in Persia; and the Jews were strongly represented in Al Medina, the Yemen and elsewhere. There can be no manner of doubt, moreover, that at some period of his life he absorbed much

teaching from Talmudic sources and had contact with some of Christianity. It seems overwhelmingly probable that his early adoption of monotheism can be traced to one or both of these influences."[21]

In Muhammad's capacity as a merchant, he had travelled as far from Mecca as Syria, Persia and Egypt and had certainly been influenced by Christianity in these areas.[22] Also one of Muhammad's concubines, Mary the Copt, was a Christian from Egypt and could well have related these stories to him.

Jesus
The Quran gives an exalted position to Jesus.

"We Muslims believe that Jesus was one of the mightiest messengers of God, that He was the Christ, that He was born miraculously – without any male intervention, that He gave life to the dead by God's permission, and that He healed those born blind and the lepers by God's permission. In fact, no Muslim is a Muslim if he does not believe in Jesus."[23]

Jesus (Isa) is referred to in the Quran as the Messiah (Al-Mashih) eleven times; He is called the Word of God (Kalimatullah) in Surah 3:45; and a Spirit from God (Ruhullah) in Surah 4:171 and Surah 58:22. Jesus is also acknowledged as a righteous prophet (Surah 6:85), and an Apostle to Israel (Surah 3:49-51).

Yet the Quranic account of Jesus' birth under the palm trees (in Surah 19:16-31) is clearly related to the Apocryphal (and uncanonical, non-apostolic) *"History of the Nativity of Mary."*[24] The Quranic account of Jesus speaking out of Mary's womb to defend her against accusations of adultery comes from the Apocryphal *"Gospel of the Infancy"*, chapters 36 and 46 (in Surah 19:29-31).[25]

In Surah 3:49 and 5:113 it is related that Jesus, as a child, made clay pigeons and by breathing on them made them come alive so that they could fly away. This was taken from the apocryphal *"Gospel of Thomas the Israelite"*, a Greek storybook. [26]

Surah 4:156 claims that Jesus was neither killed nor crucified, but that God made it seem that it was so by providing a substitute that looked similar. Evidently this theory comes from the Docetic or Gnostic sect as promoted by Basilides, a second Century heretic, who wrote almost word for word the message of Surah 4:156 in his own writings.[27]

The Trinity

Muhammad was under the misconception that Christians worshipped the Trinity as three gods – consisting of God the Father, Mary the Mother and Jesus the Son (Surah 4:171; 5:75-76; 5:119)![28] Muslims find this concept blasphemous (as do Christians!) and so attack the Sonship of Jesus. Yet this thought is foreign to every Christian and is completely unbiblical. Christians worship the One True God, the Almighty. Nowhere does the Bible speak of worshipping Mary. Apparently Muhammad misunderstood the Roman Catholic veneration of Mary and their title for her as the *"Mother of God"*. Here again the Quran is found to be based on misunderstandings and inaccurate sources.

The Virgin Mary

Surah 19:29-29 claims that Mary, the Mother of Jesus, was a sister of Aaron. Because Surah 66:12 describes Mary as the daughter of Imram (the Amram of Exodus 6:20), it would seem that Muhammad was again confused about the facts. He had evidently mistaken Mary (the mother of Jesus) for Miriam (Moses' sister) and, in so doing, has tried to persuade us that Mary was the sister and daughter of two men who lived 1500 years earlier.[29]

"The Gospel of James", another apocryphal book, was the source of the account in Surah 3:35-47, where Mary is reported to have lived in the Temple, receiving food from angels and that Joseph was chosen to be her husband by miraculous rods.[30]

The Miraj

The Miraj is the reported ascent of Muhammad to the seventh heaven after a miraculous night journey from Mecca to Jerusalem on a horse called Buraq. The details as related in Surah 17 and in the Mishkat, can be traced back to a fictitious book called the *"Testament of Abraham"*, written in the 3rd Century B.C. in Egypt and translated into Greek and Arabic.[31]

The Cave of Seven Sleepers

The Cave of Seven Sleepers is a story related in Surah 18:9;26, which bears a striking resemblance to the *"Story of Martyrs"*, a Latin book by Gregory of Tours. It is a legendary tale of Christians under the Roman persecution of Emperor Decius (249-251 A.D.) who fell asleep in their cave of refuge and awoke in A.D. 447, in the reign of Theodorus II. This story was told as an illustration of how Christianity, in disgrace and under persecution, overcame all obstacles to become the religion of the whole Empire within 200 years. In the Quran, however, the period was lengthened to 309 years and the story was related in all seriousness as an actual event.[32]

Bible Events Misunderstood

Surah 28:7-13 claims that Moses was adopted by Pharaoh's wife, whereas Exodus 2:10 (which was written 2000 years earlier than the Quran and is therefore obviously more accurate) records that it was Pharaoh's daughter who adopted him.

Surah 28:38 relates that Pharaoh ordered Haman to build *"a high tower that I may ascend unto the God of Moses."* This seems a hopeless confusion of Biblical history. Haman lived 1 100 years after Pharaoh (Book of Esther). It was not in Egypt that a tower was built up to reach the heavens, but in Babel (Genesis 11) – as well as over 750 years before the time of Moses. Furthermore, Pharaoh had nothing to do with the tower of Babel.[33]

Surah 2:249 claims that King Saul selected his small army from among a great many by noting how they drank at a river. The Bible (in Judges 7) records that it was Gideon and not Saul who did this.[34]

There are many such cases of Biblical stories being confused by Muhammad in his writing of the Quran, but these instances will suffice to show that his source was not God, nor the Authoritative Word of God, but hearsay, apocryphal legends and myths, and heretical writings. It is a great pity that Muhammad did not make more use of the *Torah* (Pentateuch) and *Injil* (Gospels). It is even more regrettable that he claimed divine revelation for second-hand stories from suspect sources.

ZOROASTRIAN SOURCES OF THE QURAN
Paradise
The description of Paradise in Surah 55:56 and 56:22-36, which speaks of *"wide-eyed houris with eyes like unto pearls, a recompense for what they laboured"*, has interesting parallels in the Zoroastrian religion of Persia.[35]

Sirât
The bridge that leads over the great gulf of hell to Paradise is called Chînarad (the connecting link) in the Zoroastrian book *"Dinkart"*.[36]

Azâzîl
The Quranic concept of the devil and several stories concerning him are very similar to Zoroastrian teachings in their book, *"Bûndahishrîh"*.[37]

EGYPTIAN SOURCES OF THE QURAN
The concept of a huge set of balances that God will operate at the Day of Judgement, as found in Surah 101:5,6 and 42:17, finds its original source in the Egyptian *"Book of the Dead"* (referring to the Judgement of Osiris) and the *"Testament of Abraham"*.

HOW THE QURAN WAS REVEALED
The Quran was revealed to Muhammad by an angel while meditating in a cave. These revelations, given over a period of 23 years, were committed to memory and recited by Muhammad and his followers and later written down and compiled.

"Muhammad himself was at first doubtful of the source of these revelations, fearing that he was possessed by one of the Jinn or spirits."[38]

Before the revelation came to Muhammad *"he saw prophetic dreams and heard unseen voices and calls."[39]* It is also recorded that Muhammad's mother used a spell to heal him from the influence of *"the evil eye"* and his nurse felt that, as a boy, Muhammad was demon-possessed.[40] The Hadith (Mizanu'l Haqq, pg.345) records that Muhammad feared that he was demon-possessed or mad, as he would shiver, foam and roar, falling into a swoon during revelations.[41]

What is of great concern to us as Christians is that we have been warned not to accept any new Gospel, even from an angel (Galatians 1:6-9). We are warned against false prophets (Matt. 24:11) and against false apostles (2 Corinthians 11:12-15).

To Christians, the testimony of one witness (in this case Muhammad) to a revelation (the Quran) is unacceptable without objective Divine proof, such as miracles and prophecy (as seen throughout Exodus before the giving of the Law, and in the Gospels before the giving of the New Covenant). Deuteronomy 18:21-22 demands fulfilled prophecy as a proof of Divine Authority for a prophet (see also Isaiah 41:21-23). Muhammad failed to fulfill any of these requirements (Surah 3:183; 6:37, 109, 124; 7:203; 17:59, 88, 93; etc.).

Muhammad dictating the Quran to his followers.

EVALUATING THE QURAN

Edward Gibbon in his classic *"The History of the Decline and Fall of the Roman Empire"* evaluated the Quran in these words: *"... an incoherent rhapsody of fable and precept and declamation which seldom excites a sentiment or an idea, which sometimes crawls in the dust and is sometimes lost in the clouds ... the use of fraud and perfidy, of cruelty and injustice, were often subservient to the propagation of the faith ... Muhammad commanded or approved the assassination of Jews ... Muhammad indulged the appetites of a man and abused the claim of a prophet. A special revelation dispensed him from the laws which he had imposed upon his nation. The female sex without reserve, was abandoned to his desires."*

Philosopher David Hume in his *"An Enquiry Concerning Human Understanding"* observed: *"(Muhammad) bestows praise upon such instances of treachery, inhumanity, cruelty, revenge and bigotry as are utterly incompatible with civilized society. No steady rule of right seems there to be attended to, and every action is blamed or praised so far only as it is beneficial to (the Muslims) ..."*

Thomas Carlyle, in *"On Heroes and Hero Worship"* described the Quran as: *"A wearisome jumble, crude, incondite (with) endless iterations ... long-windedness ... nothing but a sense of duty could carry any European through the Quran."*

Gerd Puin, a German scholar so skilled in Arabic that Yemen entrusted him with the analysis of extremely old copies of the Quran, wrote: *"The Quran claims for itself that it is 'mubeen' or clear. But if you look at it you will notice that every fifth sentence or so simply doesn't make sense ... the fact is that a fifth of the Quranic text is just incomprehensible. This is what has caused the traditional anxiety regarding translation. If the Quran is not comprehensible - if it can't even be understood in Arabic - then it is not translatable ... And since the Quran claims repeatedly to be clear but obviously is not - as even speakers of Arabic will tell you - there is a contradiction."*

Even some Muslim intellectuals such as the Iranian Ali Dashti have found the literary style of the Quran to be defective: *"The Quran contains sentences which are incomplete and unintelligible without ... commentaries ... illogically and ungrammatically applied pronouns which sometimes have no referent ... more than 100 Quranic aberrations from (Arabic's) normal rules have been noted."*

CONCLUSION

Although Islam claims that the Quran is of divine origin, I can find no internal or external evidence to support this. On the contrary, after exhaustive investigation, and after reading the Quran and other sources, I can only conclude that Muhammad based his teachings on inaccurate and untrue interpretations

An abandoned derelict mosque overgrown by the jungle in Southern Sudan.

of the Bible, derived from suspect sources. He was influenced by Eastern and Egyptian thought, Arabian customs, Jewish Talmudic writings, and legends and myths from heretical Christian sects. In addition, his teachings in the Quran are also based on revelations (which seem spiritist in nature), which he initially believed were demonic in origin.

The Quran claims to confirm the Law of Moses and the Gospel of Jesus, yet investigation shows this to be false. The Law was written about 2000 years before, and the Gospels 500 years earlier than Muhammad's time. We have enormous quantities of manuscripts of the Bible, dating long before the time of the Quran. We have enough historical and archeological evidence to support the Biblical accounts and enough manuscript evidence to show that the Bible we have today is authentically and accurately the same Word of God which was available in the time of Muhammad. Considering that the Quran accepts the Bible as the Revealed Word of God (Surah 2:136; 3:2-3; 4:136; 5:47-52, 71; 10:37, 94; 29:46; etc.), we can only assume that it is the younger Quranic accounts which are inaccurate and unreliable.

Not only does the Quran fail to bear out investigation as to whether it is of Divine origin or not, but it clearly comes from recognisable human sources at that. The misunderstandings and confusion of Quranic stories are embarrassingly obvious. Moreover, it fails to correspond with God's eternal Word revealed with many signs and wonders, detailed prophecies and confirmations in the 66 Books of the Bible.

The foundations of Islam are false and second-hand. Its sources are suspect and its roots are unreliable.

The challenge to us as Christians is that there are 1,600 million Muslims who are basing their religion on a false revelation. We are under obligation to give them the Eternal Living Word of God, as revealed in the Authoritative Written Word of God.

"Go ye therefore and make disciples of all nations . . ."
Matthew 28:19

St. Francis of Assisi proclaimed the Gospel to the Sultan in Egypt.

Chapter 7

Muhammad, the Caliphas and Jihad

To understand Islam, its Sharia law, the Islamic slave trade and terrorism, it is essential that we understand the history of the founder of Islam and his successors, the Caliphas.

MUHAMMAD

Muhammad *("the praised one")*, the founder of Islam, was born in the city of Mecca AD 570. According to Muslim legend he was born clean, circumcised, with his umbilical cord cut and immediately proclaimed: *"Allah Akbah!"* (God is great). His father, Abd'Allah died before Muhammad's birth. His mother, Amina, (a sickly woman described as involved in the occult and prone to hallucinations) died when Muhammad was only six years old. Muhammad was then cared for by his grandfather, Abdul-Muttalib, who died three years later. The nine-year-old Muhammad was then entrusted into the care of his uncle, Abu Talib, who used him as a camel driver in his caravans. Biographers have noted that Muhammad grew up as a deeply resentful young man, frustrated by his powerlessness, and relegated to the fringes of society.

When Muhammad was 25, the Ethiopians threatened Mecca. Muhammad ran away from the battlefield and became a social outcast exposed to contempt and ostracism. Muhammad then became a shepherd, the lowest social position in Arabia. Later he became an assistant to a traveling cloth merchant and this work took him to Hayacha where he met Khadija, a wealthy widow, 15 years older than he. Muhammad entered her service as a camel driver and eventually rose to become her supervisor.

When Khadija chose to marry Muhammad, his transition from rags to riches was assured. For the next ten years Muhammad developed Khadija's business, displaying skills and talents previously unrealised.

It was during this time that Muhammad began to spend time meditating in solitude, sometimes for weeks on end, in the caves of Mount Hira. It was in the year AD 610, when Muhammad was 40 years old, that he reported to Khadija a disturbing experience. He feared that he was being possessed by demons. It was then that Khadija exclaimed: *"Rejoice, o son of my uncle, and be of good heart! By him in whose hand is Khadija's soul, I hope that thou wilt be the prophet of his people."* Khadija assured him that such a virtuous man as he could not be a victim of demonic delusions, but should accept his experience as a visitation by an angel and that he should accept the call with humility and gladness. Khadija became the first believer of Islam.

From that time on Muhammad received *"revelations"* which he claimed came directly from God. Sometimes there were physical symptoms that accompanied these revelations. Muhammad would hear the sound of bells, he would perspire profusely (even on a cold day), froth and foam at the mouth, writhe in agony, jerk around, his eyes would roll backward and he would lose consciousness and enter a trance-like state.

In AD 613 Muhammad began to publicly preach his *"revelations"*. Initially, his message was simple, and Muhammad described his mission as limited to one task: *"Only to warn!"* Surah 11:12.

Muhammad preached the need to submit to Allah, and warned of the end of the world and the Day of Judgement when all would be either condemned to the torments of hell or allowed entry into Paradise.

Muhammad's ministry was received with indifference and derision by most Meccans. However, amongst his first few converts were Muhammad's slave and adopted son, Zaid, and his cousin, Ali, the son of Abu Talib and his close friend and life long companion, Abu-Bakr. The leaders of Mecca sneered at the audacity of this common man with no natural claim to authority or prestige who dared to command the obedience of his superiors. They saw Muhammad's preaching against their idols as a subversive ploy designed to undermine the established social order. Despite Muhammad's attempt at appeasement, offering a theological compromise and accommodating the three most popular Meccan deities (the moon god's daughters Al-Lat, Al-Uzza and Manat as capable of interceding with Allah on behalf of the faithful - the so-called *"satanic verses"*), the Meccans ridiculed Muhammad: Who did this pretentious shepherd think he was? This coward who had fled from the battlefield! This destitute boy who owed his fortune to marrying a widow old enough to be his mother! Sarcasm and spite were hurled at him by an increasingly hostile population.

THE MIRAJ

The painful mockery and harassment failed to discourage Muhammad. His claims grew even more extravagant. In AD 619 Muhammad claimed that the angel Gabriel took him from Mecca to Jerusalem where he prayed at the temple *("the furthest mosque")* and journeyed through the seven heavens encountering previous prophets such as Adam, Abraham, Moses and Jesus and was ushered into the very presence of God himself! All these events supposedly transpired in the course of one night, while his companions testified that his body remained in Mecca. Unfortunately for Muhammad, the temple in Jerusalem had been destroyed in AD 70. However, he was apparently unaware of that fact.

As he hoped to be accepted by Christians and Jews as a prophet, Muhammad's early revelations included positive statements about *"the people of the Book"* and Muslims were commanded to observe the Jewish Sabbath and pray in the direction of Jerusalem. Later, when it was plain that the Jews and Christians rejected his *"prophethood"*, Muhammad dropped the Jewish Sabbath and changed the direction from Jerusalem to Mecca.

In the same year as Muhammad's supposed *"journey into Heaven"* (the *Miraj*), AD 619, his uncle, Abu Talib, who had protected him, died. Then Muhammad's wife, Khadija, died a few months later. The leadership of his clan passed to another uncle, Abu Lahab, who withdrew the clan's protection from Muhammad. Muhammad became a despised and unwanted outcast, vulnerable and in an increasingly desperate and precarious situation.

THE HIJRAH

However, Muhammad's fortunes were about to change. A group of men from the oasis of Yathrib (later to be called Medina), some 200 miles north, travelled to Mecca for the annual pilgrimage to the Ka'aba, identified themselves as Muslims and promised to propagate Muhammad's message in Yathrib. In June AD 622, a group of 75 men from Yathrib came and professed Islam, pledging to defend Muhammad as one of their own. At this point, a council of elders in Mecca were being assembled to try Muhammad as a traitor. This was when Muhammad chose to flee Mecca (the *Hijrah*). Muhammad's arriving in Yathrib on 24 September AD 622 marked the beginning of the calendar of Islam - after Hijrah (AH). From that point on, Yathrib became the city of the prophet Medinnet El Nebi, which has been shortened to Medina. It was at this point, when Muhammad would finally have armed men at his disposal, that he received his first *"revelations"* permitting Jihad.

JIHAD

In Medina he was given a plot of land and a house, but he was continually short of money. Then Muhammad authorised attacks on the Meccan merchant caravans. Muhammad's first three attacks in AD 623 were all failures. However, in early AD 624 the Muslims executed their first successful ambush of a merchant caravan. Their attack achieved complete surprise because it took place in the holy month of Ramadan, a time of truce respected by even the most vicious bandits until that time. Muhammad had just received a *"revelation"* allowing warfare during the holy month of Ramadan. Aside from the loot captured, Muhammad held two prisoners captive until their relatives paid a ransom of 80 ounces of silver.

On 15 March AD 624 the Battle of Badr occurred when Muhammad's 300 men defeated a protective force more than three times their number. When 40 Meccans were killed and 60 taken prisoner for the loss of only 14 Muslims, this was interpreted as a glorious victory for Muhammad and a miracle of Allah. The prisoners were brought before Muhammad and beheaded in cold blood. One of the prisoners pleaded for his life, asking that he be allowed to take care of his little girl. Muhammad's response was: *"Hell fire!"* Muhammad then rejoiced as the man was beheaded.

Muhammad established a principle that one fifth of all the loot was always to be given to Muhammad. *"Know that out of all the booty that ye may acquire (in war) a fifth share is assigned to God, and to the apostle…"* Surah 8:41.

ASSASSINATIONS

As Muhammad strengthened his power base in Medina he ordered or suggested the assassination of various critics. This included Asma Bint Marwan, a poetess who produced poems ridiculing Muhammad and those who followed him. *"Will no one rid me of this daughter of Marwan?"* exclaimed Muhammad.

One Muslim, Umayr, that very night responded by stabbing her as she nursed her youngest child.

Abu Afak, a man over a hundred years old, who protested against the murders by Muhammad's Muslims and produced poems mocking Muhammad was also murdered at the word of Muhammad.

A Jewish poet, Ka'b Bin Al-Asharf, whose poems grieved for the victims of the Muslim assassins was treacherously slain by a Muslim who pretended to befriend the victim until he could entice him away from his home and family to murder him.

Next a Jewish merchant, Ibn Sunayna, was murdered by one of Muhammad's disciples. Then a prominent elderly Jewish merchant, Abu Rafi, was hacked to death by six Muslims while he slept in his bed at night. After this cold-blooded murder, the six men argued over which of them had actually killed the man. At this Muhammad smiled and started to check their swords. He pointed out that the one whose sword still had traces of food on the blade was the winner, for Abu Rafi would have just finished dinner before falling asleep.

The Hadith records the names of at least 27 individuals who were murdered on Muhammad's orders.

MASS MURDERS AND MASS RAPES

Muhammad arranged for practically all the Jews living in Arabia to either be killed or exiled from their homes and country. After murdering individual Jews, Muhammad expelled two tribes from Medina. The Jewish tribe of Banu Nadir was ordered to leave Medina within ten days. When they refused, Muhammad's men besieged them and starved them into submission. After several weeks they surrendered and were expelled. All their belongings and land were confiscated and distributed amongst Muhammad's supporters. The Jews of Banu Nadir were slaughtered by the Muslims two years later in their new homes.

In AD 626 when Muhammad's followers attacked the tribe of Banu-L-Mustaliq, the Muslims slaughtered many tribesmen and looted thousands of their camels and sheep. They also kidnapped some of their *"excellent women"*. Then Muhammad's followers subjected the captive women to gang rape. The Hadith records how some of the Muslims went to Muhammad with a problem. Abu Sa'id Al-Khadri remembered that they questioned Muhammad on whether it was acceptable to practice sexual intercourse with the captive women by observing 'Azl (*coitus interruptus*). *"We...desired them, for we were suffering from the absence of our wives, but at the same time we also desired ransom for them...So we asked Allah's messenger (may peace be upon him), and he said: It does not matter if you do not do it for every soul that is to be born up to the day of the resurrection will be born."*

Muhammad's revelations had already sanctioned the rape of captive women, *"those captive whom your right hand possesses"* Surah 4:24. On this occasion the only concern seemed to be whether the victim's ransom value would be diminished or lost if they were returned pregnant to their husbands. Muhammad effectively told his companions to go ahead and rape the captive women without worrying about whether or not they would get pregnant.

In AD 627 the Meccans mobilised a huge army of 10,000 men to end the threat of this traitor who was disrupting their commerce. The battle of the Ditch was a victory for Muhammad. The trenches his men had dug at strategic places around Medina prevented the enemy cavalry from being effectively deployed. As the Meccans withdrew, Muhammad proceeded to attack the last Jewish tribe in Medina, the Banu Qurayzah.

Muhammad ordered the men to convert to Islam or face death. When they refused, up to 900 were decapitated at the ditch, in front of their wives and children. The widows were subsequently raped and sold into slavery. Muhammad chose one Raihana Bint Amr as his concubine. Despite this poor woman having witnessed both her father and husband slaughtered before her eyes only hours before, Muhammad forced himself on her that night.

Muhammad taught: *"Captive virgin girls in war were made lawful for the soldiers for copulation"* Mishkat II, page 440.

THE POLYGAMOUS PROPHET

Muhammad had lived 25 years in marriage with his first wife Khadija. But after her death and the Hijra to Medina, Muhammad married at least another fifteen wives. Many of these were widows or divorcees. One of Muhammad's wives, Ayesha was six years old when she was given in marriage to him, and nine years old when he consummated the marriage, according to the Hadith.

In AD 628 Mary The Copt, a Christian slave, was given to Muhammad by the governor of Egypt, Elmokaukas. The Hadith records that the wives of Muhammad were jealous when Muhammad had no dealings with any of them for a full month, living with Mary alone.

Although Muhammad received a *"revelation"* rebuking the jealousy of his wives, he also put into the Quran a verse prohibiting his wives from re-marrying after his death.

When Muhammad married his daughter-in-law, Zainab, many of the community were scandalised. Zainab was the only wife of Zaid, Muhammad's adopted son. One day when Muhammad came to Zaid's house, he noticed the youthful beauty of his daughter-in-law's scantily clad body. The Hadith records how Muhammad exclaimed: *"Praise be Allah, who changes men's hearts!"* When Zainab reported the incident to Zaid, he rushed over to Muhammad to offer to divorce his wife and give her to him. After initially refusing this offer, Muhammad received a *"revelation"* where Allah, supposedly, instructed him to marry his daughter-in-law, Zainab.

In the ninth year after the Hijrah (January AD 630) the city of Mecca surrendered to Muhammad. At the head of an army of 10,000, Muhammad entered the city in triumph. In AD 632, Muhammad died of a violent fever at age 63, the eleventh year of the Hijrah.

THE CALIPHAS

The Caliphate was instituted as an attempt to regulate politics on the basis of the legacy of Muhammad. The Calipha was Allah's viceroy on earth, combining both religious and political power, in the tradition of Muhammad. The four Caliphas who followed in the *"apostolic"* tradition of Muhammad were: Abu Bakr, Umar, Uthman and Ali. These *"rightly guided ones"* successively ruled as Caliphas from Muhammad's death in AD 632 to 661. This has been regarded by Muslims as *"the golden age"* of Islam.

Abu Bakr, the first Calipha, was the father of Ayesha. The *"Wars of Apostasy"* that raged during Abu Bakr's brief caliphate were necessitated because the conversions to Islam by many tribes were apparently acts

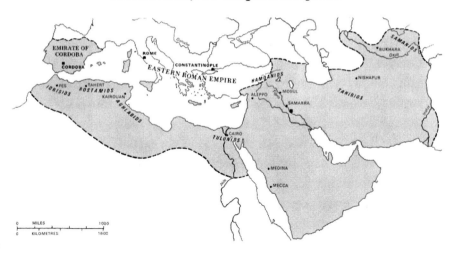

of expediency, or survival, rather than sincere or wholehearted choice. Abu Bakr died in AD 634.

The **Caliph Umar** expanded the boundaries of Islam by raiding the frontiers of Byzantium and Persia. By the time of Umar's death, Syria, Egypt and parts of Persia had fallen to the Arabs. The Byzantines suffered a major defeat at the Battle of Yarmuk AD 636. Jerusalem was captured in AD 638. The Persians were defeated in Nihavand AD 641, and the conquest of Northern Egypt was completed in AD 641. Umar made extensive use of former imperial mercenaries and military slaves who advised the Arabs in the science of battlefield tactics and military technology. In AD 644 Umar's brilliant military career was cut short when an Iraqi assassinated him while he was at prayer in a mosque.

The third Calipha, **Uthman** Ibn Affan, consolidated and expanded Umar's conquests. By trying to unify the Muslim empire, Uthman met much resistance. Many were also aggravated by his forcible standardisation of the Quran. All versions and copies of the Quran had to be surrendered under pain of death for destruction. At the end Uthman issued a new, revised, standardised, version of the Quran which endures to this day. In AD 656 Caliph Uthman was assassinated in a gruesome way and was not allowed to be buried in a Muslim cemetery.

As his wife and friends tried to bury him by night, they were cursed and stoned by Arabs. Uthman was buried in a Jewish cemetery.

Caliph Ali was Muhammad's cousin and son-in-law. From his new capital, Damascus, he attempted to consolidate the Islamic empire, amidst widespread accusations that he had been behind the murder of Caliph Uthman. With the support of Ayesha, Talha and Al-Zubair rebelled against Ali. In the Battle of the Camel, 10,000 Muslims were killed. Although Ali won this battle, he then faced an uprising from Mu'awiya, the governor of Syria, who also accused him of complicity in the assassination of Uthman. The resulting battle cost many lives, but without any decisive victory. Mu'awiya and Ali agreed to appoint an arbitrator. This undermined the authority of Ali who was assassinated by one of his former supporters.

Ali's eldest son, Muhammad's grandson, Hassan, was seen as the rightful heir. But when Mu'awiya opposed his succession, Hassan plagued by many defections abandoned the Caliphate and fled to live quietly in Medina for the rest of his life. Mu'awiya then ruled not only Syria and Egypt, but the whole Islamic empire. Ali's other son, Al-Hussein, together with most of his family, were murdered on the orders of Calipha Yazid in October AD 680. This Battle of Kerbela was actually more of an assassination than a battle. Hussein's head was sent to Yazid in Damascus.

This sealed the split in Islam between the Sunni and Shi'ite. The Shi'ites still regard Ali, and his sons, Hassan and Hussein, as the only legitimate line of succession. Hussein is commemorated as a martyr. Despite the jealousies, intrigues, deceit, dissensions, hatred and mass murders, most Muslims look upon the early period of the four *"rightly guided"* Caliphas as the most ideal model of the Umma. One that was never attained in subsequent centuries, but should be striven for.

MUSLIM MASSACRES

The first waves of Islamic conquest involved many massacres. During the Muslim invasion of Syria in AD 634 thousands of Christians were massacred.

Muslim slave traders slit the throats of stragglers.

As Mesopotamia was conquered between AD 635 and 642, many churches and monasteries were ransacked and ministers and Christians slain. In the conquest of Egypt AD 640 and 641, the towns of Behnesa, Fayum, Nikiu and Aboit were all put to the sword. The inhabitants of Celicia were all enslaved. In Armenia, the entire population of Euchaita was wiped out. When the Muslims invaded Cyprus, they looted and pillaged the homes and churches and massacred much of the population. In North Africa, when Tripoli was captured in AD 643, by Amr, he forced all the Jews and Christians to hand over all their women and children as slaves. When Carthage was captured, it was burned, to the ground and most of its inhabitants slaughtered.

At the time of Muhammad's birth, Christianity had covered all of the Roman provinces of Asia, across the Caucasus to the Caspian Sea, Syria, the Holy Land, and all of North Africa across to the Atlantic Ocean. Most of the Christians in the world lived in Asia and Africa. Europe was at that time the backwater of the Church. Some of the most famous early Church fathers were from North Africa: Clement of Alexandria, Cyprian of Carthage, Tertullian of Carthage, Augustine of Hippo, and Origen of Alexandria. Other great Church leaders came from the Middle East: John Chrysostom of Constantinople, Polycarp of Smyrna and St. Paul of Tarsus. All of these areas were conquered by the sword of Islam. **In the first century of Islam, 3,200 churches were destroyed or converted into mosques.**

"THE BLOODIEST STORY IN HISTORY"

Beginning in AD 712 the Muslim armies invaded India. Commanded by Muhammad Qasim the Muslim armies smashed statues, demolished temples, plundered the palaces, slaughtered vast numbers of Indian men and enslaved their women and children. It took the invaders three days to slaughter all the inhabitants of the port city of Debal.

At one point the governor of Iraq, Hajjaj, brought an order rebuking the armies of Muhammad Qasim for showing mercy to the infidel: *"O true believers, when you encounter the unbelievers strike off their heads…henceforth, grant pardon to no-one of the enemy and spare none of them, or else all will consider you a weak minded man."* Hajjaj demanded that all able bodied Indian men were to be killed, and that all their sons and daughters were to be enslaved or retained as hostages. At the town of Brahminabad, Qasim massacred over 10,000 men.

Ibn Warraq in ***"The Quest for the Historical Muhammad"*** describes the later exploits of Mahmud of Ghazni in the eleventh Century as passing through India like a whirlwind *"destroying, pillaging and massacring"*. Warraq summarises the effect of seventeen invasions by Mahmud: *"Mahmud utterly ruined the prosperity of the country and performed there wonderful exploits, by which the Hindus became like atoms of dust scattered in all directions…"* Describing Mathura, the holy city of Krishna: *"In the middle of the city there was a temple larger and finer than the rest, which can neither be described nor painted. The Sultan was of the opinion that 200 years would have been required to build it…the Sultan gave orders that all the temples should be burnt with naphtha and fire, and leveled with the ground."*

"... spare none of them ..."

The ancient cities of Baranasi, Mathura, Uggain, Maheshwar, Jwalamukhi and Dwarka were sacked, the populations massacred, and not one temple left standing. Will Durant in his *"The Story of Civilization"* describes the Muslim invasion of India as *"probably the bloodiest story in history"*. Historians described medieval India, until the Islamic invasion, as a most rich and imaginative culture with ornate architecture, spectacular sculptures and a complex order.

The Islamic invaders *"broke and ruined everything beautiful they came across in Hindustan"* displaying, as one Indian commentator put it, the resentment of the less developed warriors who felt intimidated in their encounter with *"a more refined culture"*. The Sultans built mosques at the sites of torn down Hindu temples and many Hindus were sold into slavery. At Somnath 50,000 Hindus were slaughtered on Mahmud's orders. The North Western region of India is called the *Hindu Kush ("the slaughter of the Hindu")* as a reminder of the vast number of Hindu slaves who died whilst being marched across the Afghan Mountains to the Muslim markets in Central Asia.

The Buddhists were also targeted for destruction, and in AD 1193 Muhammad Khilji burnt to the ground their famous library. With the Muslim destruction of the Buddhist stronghold in Bihar, the survivors retreated into Nepal and Tibet. Some escaped to the south of the sub-continent. (Some of the last remaining monuments to the Buddhist culture, four statues of Buddha, were destroyed by the Taliban in Afghanistan in March 2001).

In AD 1351 Firuz Shah commanded all Hindus to be killed and all Hindu temples to be destroyed. On the site of many of the razed temples he built mosques.

On 24 February 1568, after the Battle of Chitod, the Moghul emperor Akbar ordered the 30,000 captured Hindus to be executed. Akbar is remembered by historians as one of the most tolerant of the Muslim rulers of India. In fact, Akbar incorporated numerous Hindu and Zoroastrian festivals and practices, and was condemned as an apostate.

Shah Jahan is remembered as the builder of the Taj Mahal. He was the fifth Mogul emperor and a grandson of Akbar. What few Westerners know is that the builder of the Taj Mahal launched 48 military campaigns against non-Muslims in just 30 years. In AD 1628 he killed all his male relatives (except one who escaped to Persia). Shah Jahan had 5,000 concubines in his harem, but still indulged in incestuous sex with his daughters Chamani and Jahanara. In just one town, Banares, Jahan destroyed 76 Hindu temples. He also demolished Christian churches at Agra and Lahore. When he captured Hugh, a Portuguese enclave near Calcutta, he had 10,000 inhabitants *"blown up with powder, drowned in water, or burned by fire."* Another 4,000 were enslaved and offered Islam or death. Those who refused to convert were killed.

"UNFINISHED BUSINESS"

Serge Trifkovic in *"The Sword of the Prophet"* observes that *"the massacres perpetrated by Muslims in India are unparalleled in history, bigger in sheer numbers than the holocaust, or the massacre of the Armenians by the Turks; more extensive even than the slaughter of the South American native populations by invading the Spanish and Portuguese. They are insufficiently known in the outside world, however...Ghandi and Nehru went around encrusting even thicker coats of whitewash so that they could pretend a facade of Hindu/Muslim unity against British colonial rule. After Independence, Marxist Indian writers, blinded by their distorting ideology, repeated the big lie about the Muslim record. Militant Islam sees India as* **'unfinished business'** *and it remains high on the agenda of oil rich Muslim countries such as Saudi Arabia, which are spending millions every year trying to convert Hindus to Islam."*

SPAIN UNDER THE MOORS

On the Western front Muslim armies conquered all of North Africa, Spain and even parts of Southern France. But at the Battle of Tours (AD 732) the Franks under the leadership of Charles Martel turned the tide and drove the Muslim armies out of France. The Muslims withdrew to behind the Pyrenees mountain range which separated France from Spain. Spain under the Muslim Moors was hardly the jewel of Islamic tolerance that it is often purported to be. In AD 920 Caliph Abd-Er-Rahman III put the inhabitants of Muez to the sword. In AD 923 he entered Pamplona and destroyed its cathedral. *"Moorish Spain"* by R. Fletcher records the destruction of Cordova, Zarajoza and Merida, where all adult males were executed and all women and children enslaved.

The Surrender of Grenada in 1492 marked a final defeat of the Moors and the liberation of Spain from 800 years of Muslim occupation.

In AD 1066 all the Jews of Grenada were slaughtered. In AD 1126, the Christians of Granada were deported to Morocco. As Fletcher observes: *"In Moorish Spain, oppression or anarchy were the rule, good order and civilised behavior a fondly remembered exception"*.

Much has been made by Muslim apologists of the *"freedom of religion"* and toleration for Christians as *"protected persons"*. In fact, freedom of religion in Muslim areas only meant the freedom of Christians and Jews to convert to Islam, never the other way around. Christians and Jews were encouraged to convert to Islam, but Muslims were forbidden - on pain of death - to change their Islamic religion.

THE PACT OF UMAR

The "Pact of Umar" guided the Islamic policy towards Christians. Aside from being forced to pay "jizya", a crippling poll tax, and "haraj" (land tax) to the Muslims, the Christians were forbidden to carry weapons, to share their faith with Muslims, or even to display the cross in public.

The Pact of Umar, which all conquered Christians were forced to solemnly declare, included: *"We shall not build in our cities or in their vicinities any new monasteries, churches,…we shall not restore, by night or by day, any of them that have fallen into ruin or which are located in the Muslim quarters. We shall keep our gates wide open for the passerby and travelers. We shall provide three day's food and lodging to any Muslims who pass our way…We shall not hold public religious ceremonies. We shall not seek to proselytize anyone. We shall not prevent any of our kin from embracing Islam if they so desire. We shall show deference to the Muslims and shall rise from our seats when they wish to sit down…we shall not ride on saddles…we shall not wear swords or bear weapons of any kind, or ever carry them with us. We shall not sell wines. We shall clip the forelocks of our head. We shall not display our crosses or our books anywhere in the Muslim's thoroughfares or in their market places…We shall not raise our voices when reciting the service in our churches, nor when in the presence of Muslims. Neither shall we raise our voices in our funeral processions. We shall not build our houses higher than theirs."* (Millions of Christians for over 13 centuries have suffered under this oppression and millions still do. Compare how little freedom Christians have in Muslim lands with how much freedom Muslims enjoy in Christian lands.)

The Pact of Umar was no pact at all, but an unconditional surrender. Umar warned the Christians that disobedience to this pact meant death: *"Anyone who violates such terms will be unprotected. And it will be permissible for the Muslims to treat them as rebels or dissenters; namely, it is permissible to kill them."*

THE HOUSE OF WAR

Before the crusades began, the prominent Islamic scholar Abu Ala Al-Mawardi presented a formal blueprint for Islamic government. It reiterated the division of the world into the House of Islam where Sharia law has been enforced, and the House of

War - which is the rest of the world. According to Al-Mawardi, the House of Islam is in a permanent state of war with all others. Peace can only come with the completion of global conquest. When the Muslims are a minority community, they need temporarily to adopt a peaceful attitude in order to deceive their neighbours, but the final objective is *"Dar al Islam"*, where Muslims rule and infidels are forcibly converted or massacred. Al-Mawardi made it clear that Jihad was an obligation for all Muslims. Muslims could use tactical cease fires, but could never consider the abandonment of Jihad until all unbelievers had been subjugated.

Under Sharia law a non-Muslim's testimony is not admissible against a Muslim's. Non-Muslims could not be employed in any position of superiority over a Muslim. No non-Muslim should ever *"hold a position in which he can have power over a Muslim"*.

Islam turned its boundary with the outside world into a perpetual war zone. Muslim armies crossed the Pyrenees promising to stable their horses in St. Peters at Rome. However, exactly a century after the prophet's death, Charles Martel, the Hammer, defeated the Muslims at the Battle of Tours, AD 732.

CHURCHES DEMOLISHED, PILGRIMS PERSECUTED

In AD 1009, Kalif Hakem of Egypt ordered the destruction of the Holy Sepulchre and all Christian places of worship in Jerusalem. From this point on the Christians were persecuted even more cruelly than the previous years of Muslim rule. In AD 1065, thousands of Christian pilgrims under the leadership of Bishop Gunther were attacked by Muslims in violation of the early agreements of safe passage. The rise of the Seljuk Turks made the position of the Christian pilgrims even more tenuous and desperate.

The Christian Byzantine empire had re-conquered much of Syria and Palestine, including Antioch in AD 969. However, the Seljuk Turks invaded much of these lands and conquered Christian Armenia and most of Asia Minor. In AD 1070 they took Jerusalem and in AD 1071 they defeated the Greek emperor Diogenes at Mantzikert. Antioch fell to the Turks in AD 1084 and by AD 1092 all the Christian parishes in Asia lay under the control of the Muslims. The Byzantines appealed to the West for help to recover their lands from the onslaughts of Islam.

THE CRUSADES ARE LAUNCHED

The result was on 27 November, AD 1095, the pope called upon the knights of Europe to go forth and rescue the Holy Sepulchre and retake the Holy Land. With cries of *"Deus Hoc Vult!" (God wills it!)* thousands of knights pledged themselves to liberate the Holy Land from Islam.

It is interesting that many who excuse the atrocities of Islamic Jihad in terms of the standards of the Middle Ages, apply a double standard by condemning the Christian Crusades, which were after all only a reaction to centuries of Islamic Jihad.

Many Christians condemn the Crusades as completely against the Spirit of Christ. Certainly the word *"crusade"* does not appear in the Bible, and there are no teachings of Christ or the Apostles

Richard the Lionhearted.

commanding Christians to be involved in such crusades. However, very few people have any understanding of what was actually involved in the Crusades.

The Crusaders stormed the walls of Antioch, 3 June 1098, and captured the city.

ANTIOCH LIBERATED

The facts are that by May AD 1097 the armies of the first crusade were assembled. On 1 July AD 1097 the Crusaders defeated the Turks at the Battle of Dorylaeum. Constantly harassed by a relentless enemy suffering from the stifling heat under the weight of their armour, the Crusaders advanced through Asia Minor. On 20 October AD 1097 they laid siege to the fortified city of Antioch. On 3 June AD 1098 the Crusaders stormed Antioch and captured it. By then plague, famine and wounds had decimated their ranks and recuperation and re-supply was necessary.

TO JERUSALEM

By April AD 1099 the Crusader army was on the march again to Jerusalem. They marched through scorched earth, where all the trees, even fruit trees, had been chopped down, wells poisoned, to deny the Crusaders shade, food and water. The Crusaders also started to meet Christians and Jews who had been evicted from Jerusalem by the Muslim occupiers. These destitute refugees had lost everything and were now struggling to find water, shelter and food in a devastated area.

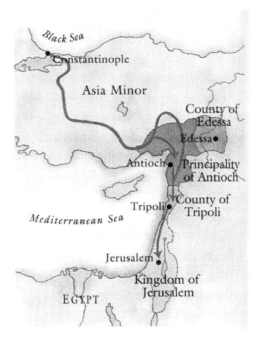

When the Crusaders reached the walls of Jerusalem they offered the occupiers terms of surrender. When the Muslim garrison responded with blasphemous comments and actions, including urinating on icons and crucifixes of Christ, the Crusaders rose in indignation and fought for the honour of their King of kings and Lord of lords.

THE CRUSADERS TAKE JERUSALEM

On 15 July AD 1099 during an eclipse of the sun, the Crusaders stormed the gates of Jerusalem and overwhelmed the vigorous Muslim defences. The Crusaders gave no quarter and slew the entire garrison, cleansing Jerusalem by the blood of these Saracens who had desecrated the holy places.

In AD 1112, with the aid of the Norwegians and the support of the Genoese, Pisan, and Venetian fleets, the Crusaders began the conquest of the ports of Syria. With the fall of Tyre in AD 1124 this was completed. By the beginning of the 12ᵗʰ Century the Crusaders controlled an unbroken, but thin, belt of territory consisting of the Kingdom of Jerusalem, the countship of Tripoli, the principality of Antioch, and the countship of Edessa.

The focus of the Crusaders was on the Holy places and the ports, so they did not attempt to develop strategic depth or create any viable economic or demographic base for the new Christian states. The crusader territory was long, thin and vulnerable to attack. To defend these outposts, the Crusaders created new religious orders of knights to provide hospitality for pilgrims and to defend the holy places from the Muslims.

The triumphant **Capture of Jerusalem by the Crusaders 15 July 1099** painting which hangs in the Palace of Versailles.

SALADIN AND RICHARD THE LIONHEARTED

In AD 1144 the Muslims counter attacked and conquered the principality of Edessa. Damascus fell AD 1154. Then in AD 1169 a Kurdish prince, Saladin succeeded his uncle as the Grand Vizier of Egypt. In AD 1171 he helped overthrow the Shi'ite Fatimid dynasty. Soon Saladin's armies were threatening the Kingdom of Jerusalem from all sides. On 4 July AD 1187, Saladin's army defeated the Christians on the shores of Lake Tiberius. He entered Jerusalem on 17 September. The Christians still held the ports of Tyre, Antioch and Tripoli.

King Richard I of England returns from the Third Crusade to an enthusiastic welcome.

When the people in Europe heard of the fall of Jerusalem, there was much outrage. Emperor Frederik Barbarossa of Germany, King Phillip of France and Richard the Lionhearted, King of England, were the leaders of this Third Crusade. Acre surrendered to Richard on 13 July AD 1191. Numerous battles pitted Richard against Saladin. Saladin respected his foes as brave warriors and a treaty was secured guaranteeing safe access for Christian pilgrims to Jerusalem and other holy places.

THE END OF THE CRUSADES

After the death of Saladin, Jerusalem was again conquered by the Crusaders in AD 1229. But in AD 1244 the city fell again to the Muslims. Al-Malik Al Zahir destroyed the Church of the Nativity in Nazareth and captured Caesarea. Caesarea capitulated under the condition that its 2,000 knights would be spared. However, once the Muslims gained access to the city they murdered them all. When Antioch finally fell to the Muslims, 16,000 Christians were executed and 100,000 were sold into slavery. By the end of the 13th Century, the last Crusader remnants in Palestine and Syria were wiped out. That may have been the end of the Crusades, but it was by no means the end of Jihad.

DYNASTIES, DECADENCE AND DECLINE

The first Caliphas had ruled from Mecca. The Ummayad dynasty ruled from Damascus for about 90 years. In AD 749 all the members of the Ummayad family were murdered, except for Abd Al Rahman who fled to Spain and founded the independent Ummayad Caliphate there. By AD 711 Islam had spread all over North Africa and Spain, and by AD 718 it was beginning to overrun Southern France. Muslim historians note that at this time a general spiritual and moral decline began to set in.

The Abbasid dynasty ruled the Muslim world from AD 750 to AD 1258. Baghdad became the new capital of Islam. Initially a small village, Baghdad was built by slave labour into the great city with palaces, mosques and impressive government buildings. This empire was totally destroyed by Gengkis Kahn in the 13th Century. The Ottoman empire was founded by Emir Osman I in AD 1301. After the massacre of the last Abbasid Khalifa and all his relatives, Turks from near the Caspian Sea began to build a new Islamic empire on the ruins of the declining Byzantine empire. Eventually these Ottoman Caliphas were ruling the whole of North Africa, the near East, India, and the Balkans of South-Eastern Europe.

THE FALL OF CONSTANTINOPLE

Muslim scholars note that the Abbasid dynasty *"drowned in decadence and luxury"* and *"had become deficient in energy and reluctant to rally in defense."* Under Mehmet II the Turks conquered the great Byzantine capital Constantinople. On 29 May, AD 1453 the sparse and woefully

When the Turks conquered Constantinople in 1453 they massacred the inhabitants - men, women and children. In Hagia Sophia 12,000 Christians werre slaughtered.

outnumbered garrison of Constantinople put up a brave, but futile, defence and were overwhelmed by the waves of Turkish invaders. The pillaging and looting went on for days. Tens of thousands of civilians were slaughtered in the streets. Turkish soldiers fought over boys and young women. The blood ran in rivers down the steep streets from the heights of the Petra towards the golden horn. The Imperial palace was looted and its treasures carried off. Priceless libraries and icons were burnt including the *Hodigitria*, the holiest icon in all of Byzantine, which was of Mary, believed to have been painted by St. Luke himself.

The fall of Constantinople on 29 May 1453 was a catastrophe heralding the destruction of Greek civilization in Asia Minor.

Sir Steven Runciman, in his *"The Fall of Constantinople 1453"* book, described the scene when the Turks burst into the greatest Christian church in the world at that time, the Hagia Sophia: *"The worshipers were trapped. A few of the ancients and infirmed were killed on the spot; but most of them were tied or chained together. Many of the lovely maidens and youths and many of the richer clad nobles were almost torn to death as their captors quarrelled over them. The priests went on praying at the altar until they too were taken... The inhabitants were carried off along with their possessions. Anyone who collapsed from frailty was slaughtered, together with a number of infants who were held to be of no value ...(Byzantine) was now half in ruins, empty and deserted and blackened as though by fire, and strangely silent. Wherever the Turks had been there was desolation. Churches had been desecrated and stripped; houses were no longer habitable and shops and stores battered and bare. The Sultan himself, as he rode through the streets, had been moved to tears."*

Many of the Eastern Orthodox Christians could not understand why no armies from the West had come to assist in the defence of Constantinople. It seemed that since the Great Schism (of 1054 between the Latin Roman Catholic church of the West and the Greek Orthodox church of the East) the Western Catholics hated their Greek brothers more than they feared the Islamic invaders.

"THE BLOOD LEVY"

Soon the Turks were occupying South Eastern Europe and threatening even the heartland of Europe, besieging the gates of Vienna itself in 1529. The Turkish Muslims even outdid the Arabian oppression of the Christians. In addition to the crippling Jizya tribute tax, the Turks demanded an annual *"blood levy"* of Christian boys in peace time. One out of every 5 Christian boys was forcibly recruited into the Sultans armies. This devshirme was introduced by Sultan Orkhan in the 14th Century.

Ibn Warraq describes the scene: *"On a fixed date all the fathers were ordered to appear with their children in the public square. The recruiting agents chose the most sturdy and handsome children in the presence of a Muslim judge. Any father who shirked his duty to provide children was severely punished. This system was open to all kinds of abuse. The recruiting agents often took more than the prescribed number of children and sold the surplus back to their parents ..."*

For three centuries, beginning in 1350, the Muslim occupiers led military expeditions into Christian villages to kidnap Christian boys for training as the Sultans janissaries. This Turkish blood levy upon the Christians has left such a deep scar on the collective memory of Balkan Christians, especially the Serbs and Bulgarians, that it continues to contribute to the hostilities of Bosnia and Kosovo. The Turkish invasions destroyed the dynamic and creative Christian civilisations of Byzantine, Serbia and Bulgaria.

A 1410 panel depicting the struggle between the Christians and the Moors in Spain.

The naval Battle of Lepanto on 7 October 1571 turned the tide of Turkish expansionism.

THE TIDE TURNS

In 1492 the Spaniards finally succeeded in freeing Spain from the centuries of Muslim occupation with the fall of Grenada.

Cyprus fell in 1571 after a heroic defence by 5000 Greek and Italian Christians who killed 6 times their number of Turkish aggressors. Unspeakable cruelties and mutilations were perpetrated on the captured Christian prisoners by the Turks.

The tide of Islamic expansionism was then turned at the battle of Lepanto on 7 October 1571 when the Christian fleet under Don John of Austria with 208 warships met the Turkish fleet of 230 warships. Hand to hand combat ensued as the Austrians flowed onto the Turkish vessels. Over 30 000 Turks were killed and 15000 taken prisoner. It was described as one of the most decisive turning points in history. When the Turks were later defeated outside the gates of Vienna, this ended the overt threat to central Europe.

CORRUPTION AND CRUELTY

Soon the Ottoman Empire began to decline into corruption and degeneracy. When Sultan Murab III died in AD 1595, his son Muhammad had his 19, brothers murdered to prevent them from claiming his throne. He also had seven of his father's pregnant concubines sown into sacks and thrown into the river. Many of his nephews were incarcerated in *"the cage"*. Sultan Ibrahim threw his grand vizier into a cistern. One morning, after an orgy, Ibrahim had all 300 women of his harem put into sacks and thrown into the Bosphorus. Only one survived by being picked up by a ship bound for France. When Ibrahim was finally assassinated, the Ottoman Empire was torn apart by corruption, nepotism, inefficiency, misrule and power struggles.

Greek Christian resistance against Muslim Turkish oppression.

A NEW WAVE OF MUSLIM MASSACRES

In the early 19th Century, after the Ottoman empire suffered defeats at the hands of Russia and Austria, and as the Greeks and Serbs mounted successful wars of national liberation, Sultan Mahmut II decided to massacre all the janissaries. The reforms and westernisation of state institutions, however, was accompanied by escalating persecution of Christians. Despite the adopting of a Western style constitution in 1839, to placate the European powers, the last century of Ottoman rule witnessed the most thorough and complete destruction of Christian communities throughout the Middle East, Asia Minor, the Caucasus and the Balkans. In 1822, the entire population of the Island of Chios, tens of thousands of people, were massacred or enslaved. In 1823, 8750 Christians were slaughtered by the Turks at Missolonghi. Thousands of Assyrian Christians were murdered in the province of Mossul in 1850. In 1860 over 12000 Christians were slaughtered in Lebanon. In 1876, 14 700 Bulgarians were murdered by the Turks. At the town of Batao, out of 7000 inhabitants, 5000 were put to the sword.

"THE SCANDALOUS ALLIANCE"

Britannia spurns the "savage and murderous" Turk. (From Punch, 1876.)

The reports of these and other routine atrocities by the Ottoman Turks were generally suppressed by the British government of Prime Minister Benjamin Disraeli, who promoted an alliance with Turkey against Russia.

Gladstone opposed the Turkophile policies of Disraeli in these words: *"He is not such a Turk as I thought. What he hates is Christian liberty and reconstruction."* What Gladstone observed 125 years ago, could easily be applied to the foreign policies of many Western governments today: the Islamophilia in the West is not so much love of the Turk,

but hatred of Christianity. As Serge Trifkovic in *"The Sword of the Prophet"* observes: *"The great Western powers - the heirs of those who had looted Constantinople in the Crusades and refused to help when the Turks were breaking through the walls with a cannon built by an Hungarian Catholic, who forced the last Emperors to forswear their Orthodox faith at the Council of Florence as the price of Western help that never came*

- those same Western powers, and Great Britain in particular, actually supported the Turkish subjugation of Christian Europeans on the grounds that the Muhammadan empire was a stabilising force and a counter-weight against Austria and Russia. The scandalous alliance with Turkey against Russia in the Crimean war reflected a pernicious frame of mind that has manifested itself more recently in the overt, covert, or de facto support of certain Western powers for the Muslim side in Bosnia, Kosova, Macedonia, Chechnya, Cyprus, Sudan, East Timor and Kashmir."

Benjamin Disraeli.

THE FORGOTTEN HOLOCAUST

The Turks slaughtered over 200 000 Armenian Christians in Bayazid (1877), Alashgurd (1879), Sassun (1894), Constantinople (1896), Adana (1909) and in Armenia (1895 - 1896). And in 1915 the Turks massacred over 1.5 million Armenian Christians.

"Passage to Ararat" describes how along the road to Adana, Turkish women were given daggers to stab dying Armenians in order to gain the credit in the eyes of Allah of having killed a Christian.

In 1881 the Turks slaughtered the Christians in Alexandria. In 1915 - 1916 over a 100 000 Maronite Christians in Lebanon and Syria were murdered.

It is no wonder that the British Prime Minister Gladstone described the Muslim Turks as: *"They were, upon the whole, from the black day when they first entered Europe the one great anti -human specimen of humanity. Wherever they went a broad line of blood marked the track behind them, and, as far as their dominion reached, civilisation disappeared from view. They represented everywhere government by force as opposed to government by law."*

SLAUGHTER IN SMYRNA

Even as the Ottoman empire crumbled and was replaced by the new Republic of Turkey under Mustafa Kemal Ataturk the ancient city of Smyrna with its 300 000 Christian population was destroyed. The burning of Smyrna and the massacre of its Christian population marked the end of Greek civilisation in Asia Minor. On the eve of its destruction, Smyrna was a bustling port and a vibrant commercial centre. The seafront promenade was a popular tourist destination.

On 9 September 1922 the Turkish mob, organized and mobilized by the Turkish army under the command of Mustafa Kemal, attacked the Greek Orthodox Metropolitan Chrysostomos. The mob ripped his eyes out,

Mustafa Kemal Ataturk.

Metropolitan Chrysostomos.

and dragged him by the beard, bleeding though the streets, beating and kicking him. Every now and then, when he had the strength to do it, he would raise his right hand and bless his persecutors, repeating: *"Father, forgive them."* One Turk became so infuriated at this that he cut off the Metropolitan's hand with his sword. Father Chrysostomos was hacked to pieces by the angry mob. The burning of Smyrna began on 13 September. The inhabitants were trapped between the flames on the one side and the Turkish bayonets on the other.

On 13 September 1922, the Turks burned Smyrna to the ground.

THE CURSE OF NEUTRALITY

Incredibly, English, American, Italian and French ships anchored in Smyrna's harbour were ordered to maintain neutrality. Some of the eye witnesses described the scene: *"The pitiful throng - huddled together, sometimes screaming for help, but mostly waiting in a silent panic beyond hope - didn't budge for days. Typhoid reduced their numbers, but there was no way to dispose of the dead. Occasionally a person would swim from the dock to one of the anchored ships and try to climb the ropes and chains, only to be driven off. On the American battleships, the musicians on board were ordered to play as loudly as they could to drown out the screams of the pleading swimmers. The English poured boiling water down on the unfortunates who reached their vessel. The harbour was so clogged with corpses that the officers of the foreign battleships were often late to their dinner appointments because bodies would get entangled in the propellers of their launches ... A cluster of women's heads bound together like coconuts by their long hair floated down a river toward the harbour..."*

While Smyrna burns, Greek Christians in Smyrna wait in vain for help on the docks.

"AN UNMITIGATED CULTURAL DISASTER"

That was the end of Christianity in Turkey. As Trifkovic observes: *"At the very time that Europe achieved its military and geopolitical advantage, the moral and religious decline that culminated in the auto-genocides of 1914 and 1939 had become evident. Having found in their grasp places their Crusader predecessors had only dreamed of reclaiming: Jerusalem, Bethlehem, Antioch, Alexandria, Constantinople - effete and demoralised European governments made no effort to re-Christianise them and, within a few decades neatly abandoned them. The moral disarmament of contemporary post-Christian Europe is now nearly universal. After World War I, with the installation of nominally pro-Western governments in many Muslim countries fashioned from the wreckage of the Ottoman empire, the West seemed to have convinced itself of the existence of benign Islam."*

Entire peoples have been obliterated in the Middle East. The Nestorians, the Chaldeans and other Christian communities were wiped out. As late as 1955 Istanbul's Christians suffered what one reporter called *"the worst race riot in Europe."*

It is no wonder that William Muir, (1819 - 1905), one of the greatest Orientalist of all times, concluded at the end of a long and distinguished career: **"the sword of Muhammad and the Quran are the most fatal enemies of civilisation, liberty and truth which the world has yet known. ... an unmitigated cultural disaster parading as God's will ..."**

INTELLECTUAL DISHONESTY

The persecution of Christians by Muslims has become a forbidden subject in Western circles. Thirteen Centuries of religious discrimination and persecution, causing the suffering, oppression, murder and enslavement of countless millions have been buried under a thick whitewash of myths of Islamic *"tolerance"*. The deceit, cowardice and silence by all too many western journalists and academics continues to facilitate the religious discrimination and persecution of radical Islam to this day.

The intellectual dishonesty of those westerners who engage in academic gymnastics to justify the invasion of other peoples lands, the looting, pillaging, raping, murdering and enslaving of whole peoples, needs to be exposed. The hypocrisy of those who justify the military expansion of Muslims, but condemn those who inflicted defeats upon these Islamic invaders, needs to be challenged. The fiction that Jihad has never been an aggressive, but only a defensive concept, should be dismissed with the contempt that

The murder in 1905 of the Austrian consul to Morocco.

such deception deserves. When Islam defines a refusal to submit to Sharia law under Islam as aggression, and when they define peace as submission to Islam, then we must know that we are not talking the same language.

SHARIA IN SAUDI

For an up to date 21st Century glimpse of Islam look at Saudi Arabia. The US State Department report on Human Rights in the Kingdom of Saudi Arabia in AD 2000 gives some indication of what is in store for those countries in Europe and Africa if Islam achieves a majority and enforces Sharia law: *"Freedom of religion does not exist. Islam is the official religion, and all citizens must be Muslims. Neither the government nor society in general accepts the concepts of the separation of religion and state, and such separation does not exist. Under Sharia, conversion by a Muslim to another religion is considered apostasy. Public apostasy is a crime punishable by death if the accused does not recant. Islamic religious education is mandatory in public schools at all levels. All children receive religious instruction ... citizens do not have the right to change their government. ... there is legal and systematic discrimination based on sex and religion."*

The Saudi religious police, (the Committee to Promote Virtue and Prevent Vice) routinely intimidates, abuses and detains citizens and foreigners. The authorities flog, amputate, execute by beheading and stoning, or firing squad. A Saudi Arabian court even ordered that the eye of an Egyptian man be removed as a punishment. Most trials are closed, and defendants usually appear without an attorney before a judge who determines their guilt or innocence according to the Sharia. Banners and adverts offer financial rewards to Saudis who inform on fellows Saudis who attend a Christian meeting or who have a Bible. Although Saudi Arabia has paid for the construction of over a thousand mosques in the United States, and several thousands in other parts of the world, no churches or synagogues are allowed in Saudi Arabia.

JIHAD SEEKS TO CONQUER OUR SOULS

As one Italian described Jihad: *"seeks to conquer our souls. That seeks the disappearance of our freedoms and civilisation. That seeks to annihilate our way of living and dying, our way of praying or not praying, our way of eating and drinking and dressing and entertaining and informing ourselves. We don't understand or don't want to understand that if we don't oppose them, if we don't defend ourselves, if we don't fight, the Jihad will win. And it will destroy the world that for better or worse we've managed to build ... it will destroy our culture, our art, our science, our morals, our values, our pleasures."*

> **"Then you will know the truth, and the truth will set you free."**   John 8:32

Chapter 8

Women in Islam

The Quran instructs Muslims to: *"Marry women of your choice, two, or three, or four; but if ye fear that ye shall not be able to deal justly with them, then only one, or any slave girls you may own."* Surah 4:3

Here, Muhammad authorises and recommends polygamy. *"Two, or three, or four…"* But then, almost as an afterthought, Muhammad recommends monogamy for those males who may have some kind of personality problem that prevents them from treating more than one wife *"with equity."* Muhammad's policy seems to be polygamy for the strong, monogamy for the weak.

A beheading in Saudi Arabia.

The Quran expressly permits sexual relations with multiple wives, and with slave girls *"whom their right hands possess"* Surah 70:30.

The Quran also assures slave owners, who force their slave girls into prostitution, that *"if anyone compels them, yet, after such compulsion, is God oft forgiving..."* Surah 24:33.

POLYGAMY DEGRADES WOMEN

Christians reject polygamy because it inhibits and in fact exterminates, exclusive, devoted love. Love between a man and a woman ought to be exclusive, otherwise it is degraded in essence to mere physical lust. No woman who loves her husband and wishes to be fully loved in return can tolerate *"another wife."*

Monogamy gives recognition, status and value to a woman. The Lord Jesus taught that *"Moses permitted you to divorce your wives because your hearts were hard. But it was not this way from the beginning. I tell you that anyone who divorces his wife, except for marital unfaithfulness, and marries another woman commits adultery."* Matthew 19:8-9

The Lord Jesus taught: *"At the beginning the Creator made them male and female, and said 'For this reason a man will leave his father and mother and be united to his wife, and the two will become one flesh. So they are no longer two but one. Therefore what God has joined together, let no man separate.'"* Luke 19:4-6

If Muhammad came to confirm the teachings of the Lord Jesus, as he claimed, why then did he undermine this principle of one man and one woman for life? And why did he make divorce in Islam so much easier (a mere verbal pronouncement) than any of the prophets of the Old Testament had ever tolerated?

THE EXAMPLE OF THE CALIPHAS

Muhammad had at least 16 wives and 2 concubines. Muhammad's successor Caliph Umar married 7 women and had 2 slave girls, Fakhiyya and Lahiyya, as concubines. The Caliph Uthman married 8 women. The Caliph Ali, to whom Muhammad had denied permission to marry a second wife beside his own daughter Fatima, after her death married 10 wives and maintained 19 slave girls as his concubines. Muhammad's grandson Hassan (of whom Muhammad declared: he

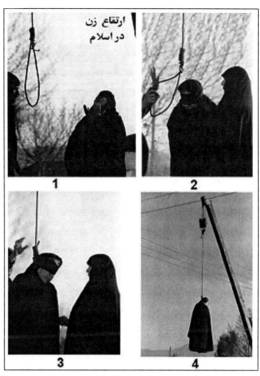

The hanging of a woman who was raped in Iran.

is the master of the youth of paradise) married 70 women and had at least 31 children. According to Bukhari in the Hadith, Muhammad sometimes had sex with all of his wives in a single night, and Muhammad boasted of himself that he had been given the power of forty men.

Muhammad is quoted in the Hadith as declaring: *"Do not ask a husband why he beats his wife...according to the same principle, do not ask a husband why he takes a second wife."*

"TEMPORARY MARRIAGES"

Muhammad also authorised temporary marriages *"for three nights"* or more. These could be contracted for some money, or a dress, or a handfull of dates. Thereafter the husband could desert the *"wife"* leaving her without any rights or obligations - even with regard to any offspring who would have no claim to inheritance or support.

By approving of polygamy, mistresses and *"temporary marriages"*, Islam denies the value of a genuine marriage based on exclusive, lifelong, devoted love. It also erodes the concept of a Biblical family. Monogamy alone gives the recognition, status and value that a woman needs, and the stability for raising children in the fear of the Lord.

"DEFICIENT IN INTELLIGENCE"

Although many Muslims are self-congratulatory about Islam's treatment of women, Muhammad once said to a group of women: *"I have not seen anyone more deficient in intelligence and religion than you...is not the evidence of two women equal to the evidence of one man?...Isn't it true that a woman can neither pray nor fast during her menstrual period?...This is the deficiency in your religion."* The Caliph Ali declared that women are evil,... *"men, never ever obey your women. Never let them advise you on any matter concerning your daily life."*

Women being beaten by the Taliban in Afganistan.

"CAPRICIOUS" AND *"CORRUPTING"*

The Caliph Umar ordered Muslims to prevent the women from learning to read and write and to resist *"their capricious ways."* The Caliph Umar once rebuked his wife for interrupting his conversation saying: *"You are a toy; if you are needed, we will call you."*

Muhammad taught that a woman is *awrat*. When she goes outside (the house) *"the devil welcomes her."* To Muhammad women needed to cover themselves with a veil, not in order to preserve their own chastity, but to preserve the chastity of the men prone to be scandalised by the spectacle. Muhammad forbad women to talk except by the permission of their husbands. Women were forbidden to use the middle of the road, to be greeted or to greet. The *"fire worshipper"*, the Jew, and the pig are listed alongside the woman as things that corrupt prayer. If a woman walks in front of a man while he is praying, his prayer is not acceptable. He then has to perform ablutions again and repeat his prayer.

PHYSICAL ABUSE OF WOMEN

In Islam, physical violence against one's wife, far from being a crime punishable by law, remains divinely ordained and practically advised (Surah 38:44 and Surah 4:15). *"As to those women on whose part he fears disloyalty and ill conduct, admonish them (first), (next), refuse to share their beds (and last) beat them (lightly); but if they return to obedience, seek not against them means of (annoyance)."* Surah 4:34

Even Islamic councils in Western countries specify how to beat one's wife. For example, the *Australian Minaret* published by the Australian Federation of the Islamic Councils declared: *"This weapon of the woman is her femininity...then beating is her remedy. So the Quranic command: Banish them to their couches and beat them, agrees with the latest psychological findings in understanding the rebellious woman. This is one of the scientific miracles of the Quran, because it sums up volumes of the science of psychology about rebellious women."*

Ahmad Ahmad in *"The Individual Guarantee In The Islamic Law"* writes: *"If admonishing and sexual desertion fail to bring forth results and the woman is of a cold and stubborn type, the Quran bestows on man the right to straighten her*

This woman, who was a victim of a rape, was buried up to her waist and then stoned to death.

out by right of punishment and beating, providing he does not break her bones nor shed blood. When your wife belongs to this quarrelsome type and requires this sort of punishment to bring her to her senses!...by the scourging which deters."

SELLING CHILDREN

The Washington Times (21/01/02) in an article entitled: "Sale of Children thrives in Pakistan" reported that girls as young as five years old are being auctioned off to the highest bidders. These Afghan girls are sold for between $80 and $100 and generally land up in prostitution or harems.

FEMALE MUTILATION

Jean Sasson in *"Daughters of Arabia"* reports on Islam's widespread practice of amputating the clitoris and sometimes part of, or even all of, the vulva from the genitalia of Muslim women, affirmed in a hadith by Muhammed himself, has led to the mutilation of millions of women worldwide.

DISCRIMINATION UNDER SAUDI'S SHARIA

The US State Department's country report on Practices in the Kingdom of Saudi Arabia (AD 2000) reports that: *"The testimony of one man equals that of two women…women play no formal role in government and politics and are actively discouraged from doing so…the government does not keep statistics on spousal abuse or other forms of violence against women, (which) appear to be common problems. Hospital workers report that many women are admitted for treatment of injuries that apparently result from spousal abuse…women are not admitted to a hospital for medical treatment without the consent of a male relative…Women may not undertake domestic or foreign travel alone…in public a woman is expected to wear an abaya (a black garment that covers the entire body) and to cover her head*

Afghan woman being shot at a soccer match.

and face…daughters receive half the inheritance awarded to their brothers…some women participate in al-mesyar (or "short daytime visit") marriages, in which the women relinquish their legal rights to financial support and night time co-habitation. Additionally, the husband is not required to inform his other wives of the marriage, and any children resulting from such a marriage have no inheritance rights…Men may divorce without giving cause…" In addition women in Saudi Arabia are not allowed to drive cars. Divorced foreign women are prevented from visiting their children. Children are always awarded to the husband or to the deceased husband's family. All these laws in the Kingdom of Saudi Arabia are based on the Islamic Sharia law.

STONING TO DEATH A VICTIM OF RAPE

The New York Times (17 May 2002) reported on the stoning to death of a young woman who had been raped by her husband's brother. The judge defended his action by saying that he had merely followed the Quran based law that mandated this judgement. The fact that the woman, Zafran Bibi, was raped, was of no consequence. The woman had accused her brother-in-law of raping her and this was a confession to a crime of *"having intercourse outside of marriage."* The *New York Times* noted that this case fitted a *"familiar pattern".*

DEATH OF A PRINCESS

When ATV in Britain and PBS in the United States were about to air a documentary based on the execution of a Saudi Arabian princess, *"Death of a Princess"*, unprecedented pressure came from the British foreign office, from the US State Department, the Saudi Arabian royal family, and oil companies to cancel the show.

JUDICIAL GANG RAPE

On 4 July 2002 the *Los Angeles Times* reported a bizarre example of Islamic justice in Pakistan. A male youth had been seen walking with a girl from another tribe. The local tribal council ruled that this outrage had to be punished. Quoting Sharia law, the local council of elders decided to punish the young boy by decreeing that his 18-year-old sister be gang raped!

RAPED IN THE NAME OF ALLAH

In 1998 Muslim men in Indonesia gang raped dozens of Chinese women in shops, homes and in the streets shouting in Arabic *"Allah Akbar"* (Allah is Great!) (*Chinese Woman Forced to Watch Gang Rape and Burning to Death of Her Sisters"* June 1998 quoted in *Secrets of the Koran* by Don Richardson)

MURDER IN THE FAMILY

On 25 February 2004, *Associated Press* reported an incident of a Kurdish refugee from Iraq who was jailed in England for having slit his 16 year old daughter's throat because she was *"too Westernised and had a non-Muslim boyfriend."* Also two cousins from a Pakistani family in England were sentenced to life for murdering a relative on the day that she was to marry a divorcee.

BURNED ALIVE IN AFGHANISTAN

The Economist (20 March 2004) reported on the phenomenon of Afghan women setting themselves alight: *"Mallali Nurzi had been thrashed by her mother-in-law once too often. She headed sobbing to the kitchen, poured petrol over herself and struck a match. Drawn by the screams, Mallali's daughter found her mother in a blur of orange flame, but the 26 year old Afghan woman still took 24 hours to die. It is hard to imagine a more agonising end, which makes the growing instances of self-immolation in Afghanistan especially horrifying. According to a local human rights group, at least 56 people have set themselves ablaze in Herat, a city in Western Afghanistan in the past year. Virtually all of them were young and married or soon to be married women, including a bride to be of 13 years…The problem may be widespread, with several hundred young women igniting themselves in Western Afghanistan every year. Mallali's grieving father, a former Army colonel, says he knows of over 80 such suicides over the past two years…there is not a village in the province where a young woman has not burnt herself to death…"*

BATTERED IN SAUDI ARABIA

BBC News Online (16 April 2004) reported on the story of Rania Al-Baz who allowed newspapers to show pictures of her swollen and disfigured face to highlight domestic abuse in Saudi Arabia. Rania said that her husband, Mohammed Al-Fallatta, beat her so hard that he broke her nose and fractured her face in thirteen places. *"It is considered a husband's right that his wife should obey him, this can involve coercion or violence and we know that the majority of cases of this kind go unreported and unnoticed"*, Abeer Mishkhas of the Saudi English language newspaper *Arab News*, told BBC News Online.

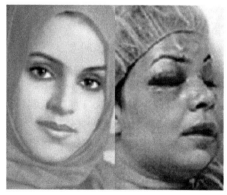

Rania Al-Baz before and after the assault.

FORCED BACK INTO A BURNING BUILDING

Newsweek (22/07/02) reported on a fire at a girls school in Mecca where every window was covered with iron bars and every door was locked. As the girls attempted to escape - breaking through a locked door - Muslim police converged on the scene to force the girls back into the burning building! Apparently many, in their haste to escape, had failed to put on the obligatory head coverings! Fifteen girls were trampled to death and forty were injured in this incident.

ABUSE, ASSAULT AND BLAMING THE VICTIM

Jan Goodwin in *"Price of Honor: Muslim Women lift the Veil of Silence on the Muslim World"* documents many horrors experienced by women in the Middle East. Goodwin relates hundreds of instances of Muslim women beaten and abused in their homes and assaulted and humiliated in public. She reports that many *"working women in Cairo have complained of being sexually assaulted on buses by men who take the opportunity ... to knead, rub and fondle female commuters .... since being manhandled is so*

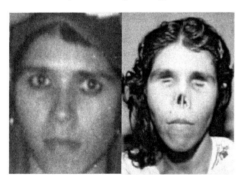

Zahida Perveen, a Pakistani 29-year-old mother of three, was disfigured when her husband attacked her after accusing her of being unfaithful and bringing shame to the family. He cut off her ears, tongue and nose, as well as gouged out her eyes.

shameful (to report) decent women suffer in silence rather than be accused of having encouraged the man." When one woman, Shahinaz was raped on a bus in Egypt, *"Fundamentalists began saying it was the girl's fault. She was wearing a skirt ... not a hijab. The media also began to blame her ... Even women said it was her fault ... she was working, not staying at home!"* Observers note that many Muslim men tend to perceive themselves as not responsible to exercise restraint because the woman is responsible not to tempt them! Thousands of Western women have complained of being groped, jeered at, insulted and assaulted by Muslim men in the Middle East.

SERIAL POLYGAMY

Iben-Saud of Saudi Arabia reported having had over two hundred wives, but maintained that since he had never had more than four at any one time, he had never sinned in this respect.

The Guardian, London (8 October 2004) reported on Kamarudin Mohammad, a 72-year-old Malaysian policeman who had just had his 52nd wedding. *"I am not a playboy"*, he said. Divorce is simple in Malaysia's Muslim majority community, since a husband can end his marriage by just telling his *wife "I divorce you"* three times. Mohammad has been a good Muslim, never having more than four wives at any one time. His marriages have lasted on average a 193 days each. But Mohammad claims that he is capable of commitment, because one of his marriages lasted 20 years.

Divorce is simple in Malaysia's Muslim majority community, since a husband can end his marriage by just telling his wife "I divorce you" three times.

A TABOO SUBJECT

The degrading and deplorable abuse of women in Islam should, you would expect, excite the outrage of women's rights groups worldwide. However, inexplicably, this has not been the case. The disgraceful abuse of women in Islam is, frankly, a taboo subject in most Western circles. Perhaps Islam's frivolous view of marriage is closer to the permissiveness of humanism than the Christian principle of the wife being her husband's closest and most intimate companion and lifelong marriage partner.

"Don't be afraid of them. Remember the Lord, Who is great and awesome, and fight for your ... daughters, your wives and your homes." Nehemiah 4:14

Chapter 9

The Challenge of Islam

POINTS OF AGREEMENT AND CONTRADICTION
Christians and Muslim Agree that:

+ God created the world and all that is in it, as well as Heaven and hell.
+ God is all-powerful. He knows everything and He is everywhere – all the time.
+ God revealed His will to mankind through certain prophets.
+ God has given us laws which should govern our lives and prevent us from doing wrong.
+ God will judge all people. Some will be permitted to go to Heaven, while all others are doomed to hell.
+ Muslims also are allies of Christians in opposing evolution, atheism, pornography, gambling and abortion.

But Islam Contradicts the Bible by Saying that:

☾ Jesus was **no** more than a prophet. He was not the Son of God (S.5:78).
☾ Jesus was a good man, but was certainly **not** divine (S.5:19).
☾ God is **not** a Trinity (Father, Son and Holy Spirit) (S.4:171; 5:75-78, 119).
☾ Jesus did **not** die on the cross for sinners (S.4:157)
☾ There is **no** atonement or reconciliation of the sinner to God by means of the sacrifice of Jesus or any other substitutionary sacrifice (S. 22:36+37).

HISTORICAL ERRORS IN THE Quran

Much of the Quran is made up of Bible stories. However, they are often distorted and misunderstood. For example:

- **Adam** and **Eve** sinned, not in an earthly garden, but in paradise. They were cast down to earth after they sinned (S. 7:19-25).
- **Noah** had only one son – and he drowned in the flood (S.11:42-43) (Cf. Gen. 6 & 7).
- **The father of Abraham** in the Quran, was Azar (S.6:74). (Cf. Gen. 11:31)
- **Moses** in the Quran, was adopted by Pharaoh's wife (S.28:7-9) (Cf. Exod. 1:5-10).
- Although the Quran recites **Moses'** confrontation with Pharaoh 27 times, not even once does it include the most integral part of the story. The Passover is omitted!
- **Pharaoh** told Haman to build 'a lofty tower' so that he 'may go up to the God of Moses'. This is obviously referring to the Tower of Babel (S.28:38). (Cf. Gen. 10:32).
- The Quran teaches that **Mary** the mother of our Lord Jesus, was the sister of Aaron and the daughter of Imran who lived 1500 years before (S.19:16-28)!

FAITH AND PRACTICE OF ISLAM

The Five Fundamentals

Muslims must believe in:

1. **One God, Allah.**
2. The existence of **angels**
3. All revealed **Books**. These are named to be:
   — The Taurat (the 5 books of Moses or perhaps the whole of the Old Testament.)
   — The Zabur (the Psalms of David).
   — The Injil (the Gospel or the New Testament).
   — The Quran.

4. **The Prophets** sent by God. Muslims believe that 124 000 have been sent to all nations, but only a few are mentioned by name. Among these are: Adam, Noah, Abraham, Isaac, Jacob, Joseph, Moses, David, Jesus and Muhammad.
5. **Life After Death** which includes a fatalistic **Predestination** and the coming Last Day of Judgement which will determine whether a Muslim reaches Paradise or hell.

The Six Pillars Of Islam
1. The open **confession** of faith *("Shahãda")*.
2. The five daily **prayers** (*"Salat"* [pronounce *"Salãh"*]).
3. The keeping of the **fast** during the full month of Ramadan *("Sawn")*. (But Muslims are allowed to eat and drink from sunset to sunrise.)
4. The giving of **alms** (*"Zakãt"'* [pronounced: *"Zakah"*]).
5. The **Pilgrimage** to Mecca at least once in a lifetime, provided one has the means for that *("Hajj")*.
6. Holy **War** *(Jihad)*.

What the Quran teaches about Jesus:
— He was born of a virgin   (S.19:20)
— He was holy and faultless   (S.19:19)
— He is the Messiah   (S.4:171)
— He is the Word of God   (S.4:171)
— He is a spirit from God   (S.4:171)
— He created life   (S.5:113)
— He healed the sick   (S.5:113)
— He raised the dead   (S.5:113)
— He came with clear signs   (S.43:63)
— He is a sign to all mankind   (S.19:21; 21:91)
— He is illustrious in this world and the hereafter   (S.3:45)
— He was raised to heaven (where he still is)   (S.4:158)
— He will come back for judgement   (S.43:61)

Chapter 10

Comparing the Bible With the Quran

The **Bible** is **66 books** written by 40 different prophets and apostles, in **3 languages** (Hebrew, Aramaic and Greek), on **3 continents** (Africa, Asia and Europe), **over 1 500 years.**

The **Quran** is one book, written by one author, in one language, in one geographic area, over 23 years.

Even the Quran acknowledges that **Jesus Christ** was miraculously **born of a virgin,** was **holy** and **faultless, performed miracles, healed the sick** and **raised the dead.**

Muhammad, however, was a trader who transported and sold slaves. He was also a slave owner. This we learn from the Muslim's own holy writings – the *Hadith.* One of Muhammad's 14 wives, Aisha, was only 6 years old when he married her and 9 when he consummated the marriage. (According to the laws of most countries in the world that constitutes child abuse.) Muhammad attacked caravans for loot and had over 600 Jewish men in Medina dig their own mass grave before having them all slaughtered for refusing to accept him as the prophet. Their wives and children were then sold as slaves. All these facts are recorded in the *Hadith.*

The authenticity of the Bible as God's revealed Word is attested to by **many witnesses,** by **miracles** such as the parting of the Red Sea, the fire that came down on Mount Carmel, our Lord feeding thousands with a handful of food, walking on the water, calming the storm, raising Lazarus from the grave and countless other events. The Bible contains hundreds of detailed **prophecies.** Our Lord Jesus fulfilled 300 Old Testament prophecies in his life on earth. The Messiah was to be: born of a virgin (Isaiah 7:14), in Bethlehem (Micah 5:2), a descendant of David (Isaiah 9:7), 483 years after the decree to build Jerusalem (Daniel 9:24-26). He would be betrayed for 30 pieces of silver (Zech. 11:12-13), by a friend (Psalm 41:9), His hands and feet pierced – crucified – (Psalm 22:16), His robe gambled for (Psalm 22:18). He would be buried with the rich (Isaiah 53:9). Yet He would rise from the dead (Psalm 16:10) and ascend to Heaven (Psalm 68:18). Unlike the Quran, the Bible is convincingly attested to by countless miracles and detailed prophecies.

There is no provision for **forgiveness** in the Quran, **no atonement** for sins (Leviticus 17:11).

Jesus Christ is the **Lamb of God** who takes away the sin of the world. In **the blood of Christ** we have full atonement for sin.

Jesus healed the sick. Muhammad healed no-one. Jesus could make the blind see. Muhammad could only make the seeing blind. Jesus made the crippled walk. Muhammad could make the walking crippled. Jesus could take a dead man and make him alive. Muhammad could take a live man and make him dead. Jesus multiplied food to feed thousands. Muhammad could divide the loot amongst his followers. Jesus could walk on the water. Muhammad could ride a camel. If you visit Medina you can see the tomb where Muhammad is buried. But if you visit Jerusalem you will find an **empty tomb.** The Lord Jesus Christ has risen. He is the way, the truth and the life. No-one comes to the Father except by Him.

Islam is a religion of **hatred** and slavery based upon a lie. Christianity is a relationship of **love** with God based upon the truth.

Quran Vs Bible

Quran	Bible
1 book	66 books
1 author	40 writers
1 language	3 languages
1 country	3 continents
Over 23 years	Over 1 500 years
No prophecies	Prophecies
No miracles	Miracles
A grave in Medina	An empty tomb in Jerusalem
No atonement	Full atonement
Hatred for enemies	Love for enemies
Slavery	Liberty

"Therefore by their fruits you will know them."
Matthew 7:20

FRONTLINE FELLOWSHIP
PO Box 74, Newlands, 7725, Cape Town
South Africa   www.frontline.org.za

PRAY FOR SUDAN

"Cush will submit herself to God"
Psalm 68:31

Chapter 11

Challenging Muslims

1. The Lord Jesus warned us to beware of false prophets – **what can you say to convince me that Mohammad is a true prophet of God?**

2. The Bible warns us not to add to or take away from His revealed Word. **What can you tell me to convince me that the Quran is true?**

3. It is good to clean your body before prayer, but **how do you clean your heart and mind?**

4. Our Lord Jesus warned us not to use vain repetition when we pray. **How do you maintain your sincerity and devotion repeating the same words 50 times a day, every day of the year?**

5. **Why are Muslims required to dress, eat and speak like 7th Century Arabians? Isn't it cultural imperialism to require everyone to speak Arabic?**

6. **Why do all Muslims pray in the same direction? Why do Muslims all bow down to the Ka'ba in Mecca? In which direction do Muslims pray when they are in Mecca? What is in the Ka'ba? Why are Muslims bowing down to a rock in a box in Mecca? Isn't that idolatry to bow down to a graven image?**

7. **What does the Quran teach about marriage? Is polygamy allowed? What about divorce? Can a woman divorce her husband? Who has custody of the children in the event of divorce?**

8. There are many consistent reports, which are disturbing and shocking, of human rights abuses and persecution of Christians in Muslim countries like Pakistan and Sudan. **What does the Quran teach about how Muslims should behave towards Christians?**

9. According to the UN Commission on Human Rights, and numerous anti-slavery societies, slavery still exists in some Muslim countries like Mauritania and Sudan. **What does the Quran teach about slavery?**

10. The National Islamic Front government in Sudan declared Holy War against the Black Christians in the Nuba Mountains and in the South killing many hundreds of thousands of Christians. **What does the Quran teach about Jihad?**

11. **In Islam how is atonement made for one's sins? How can one be forgiven?**

12. **How can you as a Muslim know for sure if you will go to Heaven or not? If God was to ask you: Why should I let you into My Heaven? What would you answer?**

13. **Does Islam recognise the rights of other religions to exist and freely operate in Muslim countries?**

14. **If Muslims became the majority in our country would Sharia law replace our present laws and constitution?**

15. **If Islam is a religion of tolerance why do no Muslim countries allow freedom of religion? In Saudi Arabia no churches or synagogues are allowed and no citizens can be a Christian - why is that?**

16. **How can Muhammad be called a prophet of peace when he engaged in 47 battles and raids on caravans in his lifetime? No Old Testament Biblical prophet - from**

Isaiah and Jeremiah to Malachi engaged in military campaigns - why did Muhammad?

17. The Saudi Arabian government has funded the building of thousands of mosques in Christian lands, yet no church or synagogue is tolerated in Saudi Arabia. Why is that?

18. Surely if the Saudi Arabians have the right to distribute millions of Qurans and finance thousands of mosques and Muslim missionaries in Western countries, Christians should be allowed to do the same in Saudi Arabia?

The author shares the Gospel and presents a World Missionary Press Gospel booklet in Arabic to a Muslim in a marketplace in the Nuba Mountains.

Intrepid missionary explorer, Dr. David Livingstone, documented and exposed the Islamic slave trade in Central Africa. By God's grace he set many captives free.

Chapter 12

Guidelines for Muslim Evangelism

GENERAL GUIDELINES FOR MUSLIM EVANGELISM

1. Avoid offending your Muslim contact by way of inappropriate dress or behaviour.
2. Be humble and prepared to listen and to learn.
3. Be hospitable. Know that Muslims must observe the 'halaal' law, i.e. they are not allowed to eat all kinds of food (particularly pork) and may be reluctant to eat at your home. Discuss this openly and try to find an acceptable arrangement.
4. Be positive. Do not enter a verbal boxing match determined to fight until one of you is knocked out! Share the Gospel lovingly. Make sure you are really understood. Explain all religious concepts and words and find out whether your listener has really understood your point. Focus on the Gospels and the words and parables of Jesus.
5. Do not compromise or be over-accommodating. Encourage your Muslim contact to test the Truth, to read the Bible for himself.
6. Do not waste your time getting drawn into arguments over Israel and American foreign policy. You are not there as an ambassador for anyone but the Lord Jesus Christ.

7. Do not just react. Muslims are likely to keep us on the defence, arguing one point after another. We must achieve a better level of communication. We should guide a conversation to concentrate on what ultimately matters - who is God, how can we know Him and how can we be reconciled to a Holy God.

8. Do not unnecessarily ridicule or debase Islam, Muhammad, the Quran or even Allah! The door may be closed irrevocably by a hostile attitude.

9. Avoid short cuts and do not try to convey the whole content of the Gospel in too short a time. A Muslim needs to be well informed. Concepts or words of a religious nature will have to be defined.

10. Ultimately this is a spiritual battle between life and death, light and darkness, God and satan. Make prayer, and not your intellect or communication skills, your primary weapon.

THE GOSPEL AND ABRAHAM

Sometimes we are asked *"Do you believe in the God of Abraham?"* And we can answer *"Certainly I do believe in the God of Abraham, Isaac and Jacob; and I believe that He is the God of the living and not the dead."*

Abraham matters to Muslims because through Ishmael they feel linked to the Father of Monotheism - Abraham.

1. **The Title given to Abraham: The Friend of God** [in Arab "Khalilullah']

   Bible: 2 Chronicles 20:7; Isaiah 41:8; James 2:23

   Quran: S.4:125 [Pickthall translation: 'the upright one']

   Ask: Why was Abraham called the Friend of God and what does this tell us about the relationship between God and Abraham? *(Note: This title tells us as much about Abraham's God as about Abraham himself!)* God can be trusted. He keeps his promises. He does not change his mind. He even wants to share His plans with His servants (see Amos 3:7) What an amazing God!

2. **Abraham is indeed the Father of all true people of God.**

   His was a special promise of God which made him to become

a blessing for all peoples on earth: Gen 12:3; 15:1-6; 17:5+19. The **Jews** considered him to be their father. Luke 3:8; John 8:33+39-59.

Every true **Christian** has reason to see himself as a descendant of Abraham: Rom 4:16; 9:8; Gal 3:7+8.

(Note: John 8:56 and Gal 3:8 are truly remarkable statements. Who could have imagined that Abraham already looked forward to see Jesus' day and received the Gospel in advance! Make sure to point this out clearly.)

3. **Abraham found approval with God only by his faith.**

Muslims are encouraged to follow the faith of Abraham: S.3:95; 2:135, 6:161

Christians are reminded to consider Abraham's faith: Gal 3:6-9 Abraham's faith was a reflection of God's faithfulness [1 Cor 10:13; 2 Thess 3:3], and this God reckoned to him as righteousness. [Gen 15:6]

4. **The promise of a son to Abraham.**

This is stated in both the Quran and the Bible.

Quran: S.11:71 ['and we gave her glad tidings of Isaac . . . ' *Note: Isaac, not Ishmael is the promised son S.37:112.]*

5. **The command to Abraham to sacrifice his son.**

To Abraham the question must have arisen: **Can such a holy and moral God ask for such a sacrifice? . . . unquestionable obedience to God's will?**

Contrast with Gen 22:1-13: Abraham was probably shocked, but in faith he obeyed – and discovered that God intended to reveal to him the glory of His salvation.

It was a threefold test: 1) to show love for God
2) to maintain his trust in God
3) to persevere in his faith

The only solution left for Abraham: **God will raise my son from the dead** [Heb 11:17-19; comp S.2:260]. Thus was Abraham's faith!

(Note: Abraham foresaw the whole Gospel:
- *his son, whom he loved dearly*
- *given through an unusual birth*
- *to be sacrificed as a sin offering*
- *his son's resurrection*
- *becomes a blessing to others*

Thus: Isaac becomes the object lesson of the atoning work of God's Son.)

1. What has God done to show His love for you?
2. Has God ever done anything for the human race to match Abraham's supreme act of love and self-sacrifice in being willing to offer his own son for God?
3. If the greatest way a man could show his love for God was to be willing to sacrifice his son for God, what is the greatest way God could ever show His love for us?

"And He opened their understanding, that they might comprehend the Scriptures. Then He said to them, 'Thus it is written, and thus it was necessary for the Christ to suffer and to rise from the dead the third day, and that repentance and remission of sins should be preached in His name to all nations, beginning at Jerusalem. And you are witnesses of these things." Luke 24: 45 - 48

A Mosque in Lusaka. More and more mosques and madrassas - financed by Middle Eastern oil money - are being built in the capitals, cities, towns and villages of Africa.

Chapter 13

Slavery Today and The Battle over History

When I was invited to lecture on: *"Slavery – The Rest of the Story"* at three university campuses in Minnesota, I expected that it would engender some opposition. What I could not have foreseen was the intensity of hostility and emotion that would be whipped up by some radical students against myself and those who had invited me.

Karl Marx declared: *"The first battlefield is the rewriting of history."* Evidently, many of Marx's disciples have been very busy on the university campuses rewriting history, rearranging reality and brainwashing students.

The University of Minnesota has 37,000 students, including over 2,900 international students from more than 130 countries, including China, India, Korea,

The author lecturing at Minnesota State University.

A Frontline mission display at the University of Minnesota.

Japan, Saudi Arabia, Pakistan, Somalia, Sudan and many others.

I had been invited to lecture at the university campus before, on the persecution of Christians in Sudan. Those presentations received some opposition, but nothing like what we received on this occasion.

Muslim students from Somalia, Pakistan and Saudi Arabia expressed great hostility, anger and emotion in opposition to my presentations on *Slavery – The Rest of the Story* . At one of the lunch time presentations in a university auditorium, the questions and answers and discussion went on for over 3-and-a-half hours after the end of the presentation. One Somalian stood up and made a long and vitriolic speech against *"President Bush's war of aggression against the people of Iraq,"* and attacked me for not dealing with this. In response, I pointed out that I was not an American citizen, that I had never worked in Iraq, that I am an African, and the subject that I had been invited to speak on was: *"Slavery – The Rest of the Story."* I had spoken on what I had personally witnessed and researched in Sudan, but I could not speak with any authority on Iraq, as I had never even visited that country.

However, I did point out that I was not aware that America was waging *"a war of aggression against the Iraqi people."* It was my impression that the Allied forces had freed the people of Iraq from one of the most brutal dictatorships in the Middle East. In fact, I asked, didn't Iraq now have the first elected government in its history? So, perhaps it would be more accurate to refer to the conflict in Iraq as a civil war where the US forces are assisting the first elected government in Iraq's history against local insurgents?

A woman, who identified herself as coming from Saudi Arabia, was most agitated. She declared that it was false to give the impression that women were oppressed in Islam. Women were *"completely free and equal."* It was wrong to suggest that Muhammad had owned slaves, she claimed, he never mistreated anybody, and Islam is a peaceful and tolerant religion of brotherhood.

I had to remind this lady that both the Quran and the Hadith confirm that Muhammad was a slave owner and a slave trader. Muhammad gave detailed instructions concerning the treatment of slaves, including that Muslim slave masters could lawfully *"enjoy"* their female slaves sexually or even hire them out as prostitutes. *"How many women can a Muslim man marry?"* I asked. *"Four"* she replied. *"And how many men can a Muslim woman marry?"* *"What's that got to do with it?"* She responded angrily. I pointed out that this indicates that there is no equality for women in Islam.

"Are you, as a Muslim woman, allowed to vote in Saudi Arabia?" *"Of course not!"* she responded angrily. *"Can you, as a Muslim woman, drive a car in Saudi Arabia?"* *"No, but Saudi Arabia is the land of Muhammad!"* *"But you can drive a car here in America? Why is it that you have so many more rights and freedoms in*

At this University at St. Cloud there was an explosion of hostility against having the facts on the Islamic slave trade presented.

America than you would have in your home country of Saudi Arabia?" In response, this woman expressed very hostile views of America and its government, prompting me to ask why she had come to study in such a horrible country, under such terrible conditions, when she could be enjoying such perfect freedom back in Saudi Arabia?

One student, apparently from Pakistan, declared that I did not deserve to live, and I should not be allowed to remain on this planet! When I asked where he would suggest I go, he exploded: *"To hell!"* In response to this I said: *"I'm sorry, but the Lord Jesus has already dealt with that, so I will not be able to join you."*

One of the most surprising aspects of my visit to the university campuses in Minnesota was the hostility of many university lecturers against Christianity and America. As a missionary who has spent almost 25 years ministering to restricted access areas in Africa, I expect opposition from Muslims and Marxists. However, as experienced during these campus outreaches in Minnesota, some of the most fervent opposition we received came from nominal Christians who seem either infatuated with, or in fear of, Islam. They seemed most antagonistic towards Biblical Christianity and even hostile to the Christian civilisation, which they benefit from.

One university professor stood up during the question and answer time and declared that he was most disappointed with my presentation. It was *"the most bigoted, narrow-minded lecture"* he had ever heard in his life. He had brought his students from his history class to hear me, expecting that I would speak about the American involvement in the slave trade. He didn't understand why I would have dealt with such *"hurtful"* and *"offensive"* material as the Muslim involvement in the slave trade. Why hadn't I given more time and attention to America's involvement?

To this I had to respond that surely the advertised title of my presentations: *Slavery – The Rest of the Story* should have made it abundantly clear that it was not my purpose to come to America to repeat again what most Americans are so familiar with, and what ended over 150 yeas ago. As an African missionary, who had witnessed the ongoing slave trade in Sudan today, I had undertaken a research

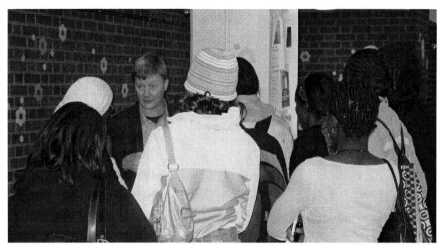
Discussions with Muslim students continued for hours after the lectures.

project into the history of slavery in Africa and the result was the book: *Slavery, Terrorism and Islam − The Historical Roots and Contemporary Threat −* on which these lectures had been based.

The American involvement in the slave trade lasted for less than 3 centuries; however, the Muslim involvement in the slave trade has continued for 14 centuries and is still continuing to this day. Considering that 95% of the African slaves who were transported across the Atlantic went to South and Central America, mainly to Portuguese, Spanish and French possessions, and that less than 5% of the slaves who crossed the Atlantic went to the United States, it was remarkable that the vast majority of academic research, films, books and articles concerning the slave trade concentrated only on the American involvement, as though slavery was a uniquely American aberration. The vastly great involvement of Portugal, Spain and France seems to be largely ignored. Even more so the far greater and longer running Islamic slave trade into the Middle East has been so ignored as to make it one of history's best-kept secrets.

Now, I pointed out, if I had concentrated on the American slave trade, that would have been ignorant, bigoted and prejudiced.

A Saudi Arabian student argues with the author.

Numerous Sudanese university students stood up to confirm the truth of my presentations, that there was indeed slavery continuing in Sudan today. *"It is a fact! No one can deny it! The facts and the documentation are there, for anyone to see. We ourselves have seen and experienced it. The Americans are very honest and admit their involvement in slavery over 150 years ago. Why can't you Muslims be honest and admit what is going on in your own countries, and deal with it?"* challenged one student from Sudan.

Another man from Mexico spoke up: *"My ancestors were the Aztecs. We were the biggest slave traders, and the slaves were used for human sacrifice - to make the sun rise each day! Our Aztec priests ripped out the beating hearts from living slaves who were sacrificed in our temples. Men were enslaved and sacrificed like that. I don't like it. I am not proud of it, but it is a fact. It is part of our history. We have to face up to it. And the slavery and human sacrifice in Mexico only stopped when Christianity came and brought it to an end. That is the fact of history. When are the Arabs going to face up to the facts of their own history, and to what is going on in many Muslim countries today? When are they going to rise up like the Christians to bring this slavery in their own countries to an end?"*

The atmosphere in the university auditorium was electric, as various students and some lecturers took part in the very vigorous question and answer time, and debating, arguing and discussing these volatile topics.

At one of the university campus meetings, I was still surrounded by about 10 students, including some from Somalia, Pakistan and Saudi Arabia, 4 and a half hours after the beginning of the presentation.

Suddenly I realised that all the discussion had stopped and everyone was silent. They were all listening to me. After hours of shouting and argument, it was an eerie experience as I related the parables of Christ, particularly of the two men who went up to the Temple to pray: the one was a religious leader, a Pharisee; and the other was a tax collector – a sinner. I related the contrast between these two men. The one self-righteous, convinced of his own goodness and moral superiority, and the other man humbled and repentant only crying out: *"Lord, have mercy on me, a sinner!"* Then I asked them which of these two men were justified in God's sight? Whose prayer did the Lord find acceptable? The Muslim students remained silent as one of the Christians responded: *"The tax collector, because he was repentant."* This seemed to shock the Muslims as they would have thought that the religious leader, with his fasting, was the righteous one.

I also had the opportunity to share the Gospel in the story of Abraham being willing to sacrifice his son and how God Himself provided the lamb. I pointed them to Jesus, who is the Lamb of God, who takes away the sins of the world (John 1:29). He died in our place, the Just for the unjust.

After all the heated emotions, anger and shouting, it was an extraordinary experience to be able to communicate calmly and clearly the Gospel presentation to these Muslims who had been so emotive and hostile for so many hours.

My respect was greatly increased for the campus ministries that have to work in such volatile and hostile environments on a daily basis. Campus ministries, such as Maranatha, are laying a foundation for righteousness for future generations. On a daily basis they are seeking to evangelise in dorm rooms, class rooms and offices throughout the university community. With guest speakers like myself, and through men's and women's Bible studies, prayer meetings, contact tables and outreaches, they are challenging the present politically correct propaganda of Humanism and the New Age Movement with the life changing power of the Gospel of Salvation and Jesus Christ alone.

My host, Rev. Bruce Harpel, who founded Maranatha Christian Fellowship over 25 years ago, explains: *"In the classroom, students are indoctrinated to think that truth is relative, that there are no absolutes, and what is right and wrong are determined by the individual and society."*

"Drinking, drugs, sexual immorality, and lack of accountability lead some students to self destruction. The student usually exits college much more wounded and addicted to sin than when he/she entered. Many times students who were raised in Christian homes abandon their beliefs as they are challenged by opposing worldviews. When these students return to their respective towns, cities, and countries, this bondage to sin is transfused into the bloodstream of society. We see more white-collar crime, violence, sexually transmitted diseases, abortions, suicide, divorce, depression and despair in society than ever before. The University is truly a mission field and that is why we are here. To ignore campus ministry is to surrender the culture to the enemy."

"Where the Spirit of the Lord is, there is freedom."
2 Corinthians 3:17

Chapter 14

Muslim Evangelism in Universities

When Maranatha Christian Fellowship again organized a series of public meetings for me in three universities in Minnesota, it was on *The Crusades and Jihad*.

Previously I'd been invited to speak at the universities in Minnesota on *Sudan*, and on *Slavery – The Rest of The Story*. These presentations had engendered a lot of controversy and attention, particularly from Muslim students. These university meetings on *The Crusades and Jihad* received even more opposition from Muslim and Atheist students.

The author presents The Crusades vs Jihad at the University of Minnesota.

MINISTERING TO MUSLIMS

The first meeting at Minnesota State University in Mankato was packed out, with standing room only, and with people sitting on the floor. Many

Muslim students insulted and threatened Dr. Peter Hammond for reporting the facts on Jihad.

Muslims came and participated in the question and answer session afterwards. The discussion time was lively, often highly emotional and volatile. Students who identified themselves as from Saudi Arabia, Somalia, Pakistan, Iran, Syria and Sudan participated in the often tumultuous discussion time.

TERRORISM DEFENDED

After numerous students claiming that Islam was always peaceful and tolerant, that no Muslims take these Jihad verses literally, and that no one who participates in terrorism or violence could possibly be a true Muslim, I asked one student whether she regarded Osama Bin Laden as a true Muslim or not. *"Of course he is a Muslim!"* came her response. *"Even though Osama Bin Laden has planned and organized terrorist attacks which have led to the death of thousands of American civilians, do you recognize Osama Bin Laden as a Muslim?" "Yes, of course, he is a Muslim."* She asserted. *"We cannot judge him!"* agreed other Muslim students. Uniformly, the large group of Muslim students nodded their heads and agreed and verbally asserted that of course Osama Bin Laden was a true Muslim.

SUICIDE BOMBING JUSTIFIED

Then I questioned them concerning the Al Queda suicide bombers: *"Are the suicide bombers true Muslims?"* Incredibly, these Muslim students defended the suicide bombers, not only in Israel, but in England as well! They claimed that because of what Israel had done in occupying the West Bank, and Gaza, the suicide bombers were justified in blowing themselves up in order to kill as many Jews as possible.

"But what about the civilians in London?" I asked. *"Surely you cannot support suicide bombing in London?"* Yet, the Muslim students persisted in defending the suicide bombers, even in London, asserting that England was *"a Crusader state!"* and that I deserved to die because I was *"a white male!"*

After so many passionate assertions of how Islam is only peaceful, and always tolerant, and that they never support violence or terrorism, it was shocking to those present to hear those very same Muslims passionately defend Osama Bin Laden and Al Queda's terrorism and suicide bombers, including those who attacked the commuters in the London underground.

FIRSTHAND FROM SUDAN

After many Muslim had insulted and threatened me, numerous black Christian students from Sudan stood up and defended my presentation, with personal testimonies of their experiences suffering under Islamic Jihad in Sudan. *"What our brother has said, is true. We have seen it. This is the truth. Jihad is a reality in Sudan. Many black Christian men and women have been murdered in Sudan in the name of Jihad, in the name of Allah and Muhammad, and many children enslaved in Sudan."*

A TESTIMONY OF SALVATION IN CHRIST

Then a young woman from Azerbaijan presented her dynamic testimony. Vera had been raised a Muslim in this 99% Islamic state. She testified how the Lord had saved her and healed her and brought 20 other Muslims to Christ through her testimony in Azerbaijan. She testified of persecution, and being imprisoned and threatened for her faith.

The tension in the lecture hall was absolutely electric. You could have heard a pin drop after Vera's radiant testimony. When the meeting closed, numerous evangelistic discussions ensued, with Christian students, including the Sudanese believers, interacting with the Muslim visitors and sharing the Gospel with them most passionately.

ONLY A MUSLIM CAN QUOTE FROM THE QURAN

At the University of Minnesota in Minneapolis, the venue was also packed out with large numbers of Muslims coming in throughout the presentation. The discussion time at the end was vibrant and volatile. Numerous members of the local Atheist Society participated, along with the Muslims, in challenging, insulting and threatening me. When I responded

After demanding more evidence that the Quran taught Jihad, this student insisted that only a Muslim could be permitted to quote from the Quran!

by quoting from both the Quran and the Bible, and clearly presenting the facts of history, numerous of the Muslims asserted that I had no right to quote from the Quran as I wasn't a Muslim. There were many more emotional outbursts and some extreme hatred for Christianity expressed by some of the students in attendance at these meetings.

This Muslim student thought that Soviet dictator Joseph Stalin was a Christian!

THE ATHEIST HOLOCAUST

The question and answer time became explosive. There was lots of screaming and shouting, and wildly insane comments. One student stood up and declared: *"Look at what Christians like Joseph Stalin have done in Russia!"* I had to respond: *"Excuse me, do I understand you correctly? Are you suggesting that Joseph Stalin, the Dictator of Russia, was a Christian?!"* When the Muslim confirmed that yes, that was exactly what he was saying, I had to remind him: *"But Joseph Stalin was an Atheist who destroyed over 48,000 churches and murdered millions of Christians. Communism is inherently Atheistic. Atheism, materialism and economic determinism are the three pillars of communism. Stalin declared that evolution prepares the way for revolution."*

The head of the Atheist Society exploded that it was outrageous for me to suggest that millions of people had been killed in the name of Atheism. I responded: *"But, of course, that is the fact. Over 160 million people were killed in the 20th Century alone, in the name of Atheism. Secular Humanist governments, such as in the Soviet Union, Red China, Cambodia, North Korea, Ethiopia, Mozambique, Angola, Cuba and Zimbabwe, in the name of Atheism, have killed millions of their own citizens, in the name of Atheism and Darwinian social theory."*

The author answers the questions of an Iranian student.

EVANGELISING MUSLIMS

As on every other occasion, when the meeting officially ended, the ministry continued with the Maranatha Christian Fellowship students well placed throughout the room to engage in effective evangelistic conversations with the visiting Muslims, Atheists and assorted pagans. These discussions went on for hours.

Specially prepared evangelistic DVDs with the testimonies of Muslims converted to Christ were distributed to interested students. There was much interest in our evangelistic and missions literature and CDs and numerous of the Muslim students requested Bibles and Christian films such as the *Jesus* film in their own languages.

After each meeting I had opportunities to personally share the Gospel with students from Iran, Saudi Arabia, Pakistan, Somalia, Sudan and Syria.

"But sanctify the Lord God in your hearts, and always be ready to give a defence to everyone who asks you to give a reason for the hope that is in you, with meekness and fear."   1 Peter 3:15

Chapter 15

The Crusades and Jihad

Back in 1999 while our mission was being bombed by the National Islamic Front government in Sudan, fellow missionaries were organising "Reconciliation Walks" to the Middle East to apologise for "The Crusades". At the time, as our church services were under aerial and artillery bombardment by Jihadists, it seemed rather bizarre. Therefore I undertook a study of the crusades and Jihad.

The author and two pastors examine the damage to Fraser Cathedral in Lui. It was bombed by the Sudan Air Force just after Christmas 2000. This was the third time this landmark church - the birthplace of Christianity in Moruland - had been destroyed by Muslim forces. Yet each time it has been rebuilt.

Anin Maalouf in "The Crusades through Arab eyes" claims that the Crusaders' conquest of Jerusalem in 1099 was *"The starting point of a millennial hostility between Islam and the West."* Islamic scholar John Esposito blames the Crusades for disrupting *"Five centuries of peaceful coexistence elapsed before political events and an imperial papal power-play led to a centuries long series of so called Holy Wars that pitted Christendom against Islam and left an enduring legacy of misunderstanding and distrust." ("Islam: The Straight Path"* OUP).

WHAT PRECEDED THE CRUSADES?

However the Crusades only started after five centuries of Islamic Jihad had conquered and annihilated, or forcibly converted, over two thirds of what had formerly been the Christian world. Shortly after the Islamic conquest of Jerusalem, in 638, Christian pilgrims were harassed, massacred, and early in the 8th Century, 60 Christian pilgrims from Amoriem were crucified.

Christian women grieve the murders of their husbands and sons, as the Muslims show them a pile of severed heads.

The Muslim governor of Caesarea seized a group of pilgrims from Iconium and had them all executed. Muslims extorted ransom money from Pilgrims, and threatened to ransack the most holy churches in Christendom such as the Church of the Resurrection - if they didn't pay exorbitant taxes. In the 8th Century a Muslim ruler banned all displays of the Cross in

Jerusalem. He also increased the penalty tax (*Jizya*) and forbade Christians to engage in any religious instruction, even of their own children! In 772, the Calipha al Mansur ordered the hands of all Christians and Jews in Jerusalem to be branded.

In 789, Muslims beheaded a monk in Bethlehem, plundering the monastery and slaughtering many more Christians. In 923, a new wave of destruction of churches was launched by the Muslim rulers. In 937, Muslims went on a rampage in Jerusalem on Palm Sunday plundering and destroying

Christian women captives were degraded by Muslim invaders.

the Church of Calvary and the Church of the Resurrection.

In 1004 the Fatimid Calipha Abu Ali al–Mansur al–Hakim unleashed a violent wave of church burning and destruction, confiscation of Christian property, and ferocious slaughter of both Christians and Jews. Over the next ten years, thirty thousand churches were destroyed and vast numbers of Believers were forcibly converted or killed.

In 1009, Al-Hakim ordered that the most holy churches in Christendom – the Church of the Holy Sepulchre and the Church of the Resurrection in Jerusalem - be destroyed. He heaped humiliating and burdensome decrees upon Christians and Jews forcing Christians to wear heavy crosses around their necks, and Jews to have blocks of wood in the shape of a calf around their necks. Ultimately, he ordered Christians and Jews to either accept Islam or flee his areas of control.

Christians remained in a precarious position and under threat throughout the Middle East. When the Seljuk Turks swept into Jerusalem in 1077 they murdered over three thousand people, including many Christians. It was at this point that the Christian Emperor of Byzantium, Alexius I, appealed for help to the Western churches.

Pope Urban II challenged the knights of Europe at the Council of Clermont in 1095: *"The Turks and Arabs have attacked our brethren in the East and have conquered the territory of Romania (the Greek Empire) as far as the shore of the Mediterranean and the Hellespont…have occupied more and more of the lands of those Christians and have overcome them in seven battles. They have killed and captured many and have destroyed the churches and devastated the Empire. If you continue to permit them to continue thus for a while with impunity, the faithful of God will be much more widely attacked by them. On this account I…persuade all people of whatever rank, foot soldiers and knights, poor and rich, to carry aid promptly to those Christians…"*

Nowhere was the call for the launch of the Crusades talking about either conquest or conversion, they were merely to remove the Islamic invaders from the lands that had previously been Christian, to restore religious freedom to the Holy Lands.

MYTHS AND MISCONCEPTIONS

The politically correct dogma that the Crusades were unprovoked, imperialist actions against the peaceful, indigenous Muslim population is simply not accurate. Such propaganda reflects a hostility for Western civilization, and often against Christianity itself, rather than any actual historical research.

Similarly, the characterization of the Crusaders as greedy for loot, only out for personal gain, is simply out of touch with reality. Those who participated in the Crusades saw it as an act of sacrifice rather than of profit. The Crusades were in fact prohibitively expensive. Many Crusaders had to sell their property to raise money for the long journey to the Holy Land and knew that their chances of returning alive were slight. Most who did manage to survive and return came back with nothing material to show for their efforts.

Similarly the modern PC myth that the Crusaders attempted to forcibly convert Muslims to Christianity is a politically motivated fantasy. Search as one might through the writings and records of the Crusaders, one will not find any mention of Crusaders seeking to convert the Saracens or the Turks. The Crusaders saw themselves as Pilgrims seeking to recapture and liberate Christian lands from vicious invaders.

Muslim Turks crucify a Christian on the walls of Jerusalem - in full view of the Crusaders.

Even Maalouf in *The Crusades Through Arab Eyes*, reports the observations of Spanish Muslim Ibn Jubayr who traversed the Mediterranean on his way to Mecca in the early 1180s and found that the Muslims were far better off in those lands controlled by the Crusaders than they were in Muslim ruled lands. And that Muslims preferred to live in the Crusader realms as those lands were more orderly and better managed.

Ibn Jubayr wrote: *"Whose lands were efficiently cultivated. The inhabitants were all Muslims. They live in comfort with the Franks – may God preserve them from temptation! Their dwellings belong to them and all their property is unmolested. All their regions, patrolled by the Crusaders in Syria, are subject to the same system: The land that remains, the villages and farms, have remained in the hands of the Muslims. Now, doubt invests the hearts of a great number of these men when they compare their lot to that of their brothers living in Muslim territories. Indeed, the latter suffer from the injustices of their co-religionists, whereas the Franks act with equity."*

Crusaders commit their enterprise to God in prayer.

The Crusades have often been portrayed as European Colonialism, but the Crusader states were not ruled from Western Europe. The governments they established did not answer to any Western power. Nor did the Crusader rulers siphon off the wealth of their lands and send it back to Europe. No streams of settlers came from Europe to settle in these states, which were established only in order to provide permanent protection for Christians in the Holy Land.

THE MERCIFUL SALADIN

The presentation of Muslim commanders such as Saladin as merciful and magnanimous is a myth. When Saladin captured the Crusaders at Hattim on 4 July 1187, he ordered the mass execution of all the Christians: *"They should be beheaded in accordance with Quran 47:4 'When you meet the unbelievers on the battlefield, strike their necks'"* Saladin's secretary Imad reported, *"With him were a whole band of scholars and Sufis and a certain number of devout men and aesthetics; each begged to be allowed to kill one of them and drew their swords and rolled back their sleeves. Saladin, his face joyful, was sitting on his dais; the unbelievers showed black despair."*

In 1148, the Muslim Commander Nur ed–Din ordered the slaughter of every Christian in Aleppo.

Richard the Lionhearted attacks Saladin's army at the battle of Arsuf.

In 1268, when Mamluk Sultan Baybars seized Antioch, he ensured that all the men were slaughtered, the women sold into slavery, the crosses in every church smashed, the Bibles torn and burned, the graves of Christians desecrated. Every monk, priest and deacon was dragged to the altar and had their throats slit where a mass had previously been celebrated, the Church of Saint Paul and the Cathedral of Saint Peter were destroyed and the bodies of the Christians burned.

When, on 29 May 1453, the greatest city in the world of that time, Constantinople, was conquered by the Jihadists, the Muslims *"slew everyone that they met in the streets, men, women and children without discrimination. The blood ran in rivers down the steep streets from the heights of Petra toward the golden horn"*. The Muslim soldiers even entered the Hagia Sophia, and slaughtered thousands of Christians worshipping in what was then the largest church in the world.

WHAT DID THE CRUSADES ACHIEVE?

The Crusades bought Europe time. From the first century of Islam Muslim armies were invading Europe. Spain suffered under Islamic occupation for 8 centuries. In the 14th Century, Greece, Bulgaria, Serbia, Macedonia, Albania and Croatia fell to Muslim invasions.

In 1426 the Egyptian Mukluks conquered Cyprus. In 1395 the Muslims conquered Nicopolis on the Danube River. In 1444 the Muslim armies seized Varna in Hungary. In 1456 the Turks besieged Belgrade, and even tried to conquer Rome, but were thrown back. The Muslims first attempted to seize Vienna in 1529. As late as 11 September 1683 Muslim armies besieged Vienna, but were routed by 30,000 Polish Hussars (cavalrymen) led by Poland's King Jan III Sobieski.

WERE THE CRUSADES A FAILURE?

The constant depiction of the Crusades as a failure is not justified by the historical record. The Crusades succeeded in seizing the initiative, throwing the Muslim invaders onto the defensive, for the first time after five centuries of attack. The Crusaders bought Europe time – centuries in fact.

At a critical time, the Crusades united a divided Europe, and threw the Muslim invaders back, bringing a peace and security to Europe that had not been known for centuries. As a result of the tremendous sacrifices of the Crusaders, Christian Europe experienced Spiritual Revival and Biblical Reformation which inspired a great resurgence of learning, scientific experimentation, technological advancement, and movements that led

Florine of Burgundy engages the Muslims in combat.

to greater prosperity and freedoms than had ever been known in all of history.

For a picture of what Europe might be like today had Islam succeeded in conquering it, one can look at the previously Christian civilisations of Egypt and what is today called Turkey. The Copts in Egypt now make up just 10% of the total Egyptian population, and are severely oppressed. What is today called Turkey was once the vibrant Christian Byzantine Empire, the economic and military superpower of its day. Today the Christian civilization which had flourished there for a thousand years has all but been extinguished. The population of the last Christian city in Asia, Smyrna, was massacred by the Turkish Army in 1922.

Godfrey leads the crusaders through the walls to liberate Jerusalem, 1099.

The classic Hollywood version of the Crusades as depicted in the $150 million *Kingdom of Heaven* epic was produced in consultation with groups such as the Council on American – Islamic Relations.

Professor Jonathan Riley-Smith, author of *A Short History of The Crusades* described the film as *"Rubbish!...it's not historically accurate at all... it depicts the Muslims as sophisticated and civilized and the Crusaders are all brutes and barbarians. It has nothing to do with reality."*

The Crusades ended over 700 years ago. Islamic Jihad continues to this day.

The popular misconceptions about the crusades are that these were aggressive wars of expansion fought by religious fanatics in order to evict Muslims from their homeland, and force conversions to Christianity. However the historical record does not support those assertions.

A REACTION TO JIHAD

The crusaders were reacting to over four centuries of relentless Islamic Jihad, which had wiped out over 50% of all the Christians in the world and conquered over 60% of all the Christian lands on earth – before the crusades even began . Many of the towns liberated by the crusaders were still over 90% Christian when the crusaders arrived. The Middle East was the birthplace of the Christian Church. It was the Christians who had been conquered and oppressed by the Seljuk Turks. So many of the towns in the Middle East welcomed the crusaders as liberators.

Far from the crusaders being the aggressors, it was the Muslim armies which had spread Islam from Saudi Arabia across the whole of Christian North Africa into Spain and even France within the first century after the death of Muhammad. Muslim armies sacked and slaughtered their way across some of the greatest Christian cities in the world, including Alexandria, Carthage, Antioch and Constantinople. **These Muslim invaders destroyed over 3,200 Christian churches just in the first 100 years of Islam.**

The Crusaders attributed their first great victory at Nicea to Divine intervention.

DEFENSIVE WARS

As Professor Thomas Madden in *The Real History of the Crusades* points out: *"The crusades to the East were in every way defensive wars. They were a direct response to Muslim aggression – an attempt to turn back, or defend against, Muslim conquests of Christian lands. Christians in the 11th Century were not paranoid fanatics. Muslims really were gunning for them...Islam was born in war and grew the same way. From the time of Muhammad, the means of Muslim expansion was always by the sword...Christianity was the dominant religion of power and wealth...The Christian world therefore was a prime target for the earliest Caliphas and it would remain so for Muslim leaders for the next thousand years...The crusades...were but a response to more than four centuries of conquests in which Muslims had already captured over two thirds of the Christian world."* **Without the Crusades it is questionable whether Europe or America would even exist.**

THINKING THE UNTHINKABLE

As the London Telegraph pointed out: *"A more realistic view of history requires less retrospective fantasy and more brain work. It means forcing your head around to see what motivated men and women centuries ago. Try to think the unthinkable – that the Crusaders were right, and that we should be grateful to them."*

CHRISTIAN LOVE AND SELF SACRIFICE

Professor Jonathan Riley-Smith explains that crusading was *"an act of love"* for one's neighbour. An act of mercy to right a terrible wrong. As one church leader wrote to the Knights Templar: *"You carry out in deeds the words of the Gospel, 'greater love than this hath no man, than that he lay down his life for his friends'."*

Professor Riley-Smith points out that the goals of the crusades were firstly to rescue the Christians of the East: *"Many thousands of Christians are bound in slavery and imprisoned by the Muslims and tortured with innumerable torments."* And secondly the liberation of Jerusalem and other places made holy by the life of Christ.

The Medieval crusaders saw themselves as pilgrims, restoring to the Lord Jesus Christ His property. *"The Crusaders' conquest of Jerusalem, therefore, was not colonialism, but an act of restoration and an open declaration of one's love of God...It is often assumed that the central goal of the crusades was forced conversion of the Muslim world. Nothing could be further from the truth. From the perspective of Medieval Christians, Muslims were the enemies of Christ and His Church. It was the Crusaders' task to defeat and defend against them. That was all. Muslims who lived in crusader won territories were generally allowed to retain their property and livelihood and always their religion."*

AGAINST ALL ODDS

When we think about the Middle Ages, we inevitably view Europe in the light of what it became rather than what it was. The fact is that the superpower of the Medieval world was

200 Knights attacked 20 000 Saracens.

Islam, not Christendom. The crusades were a battle against all odds with impossibly long lines of supply and cripplingly inadequate logistics. It was a David against Goliath enterprise from the beginning. The chances of success for the first crusade were highly improbable. They had no leader, no chain of command, no supply lines and no detailed strategy. The first crusade consisted simply of thousands of dedicated warriors marching deep into enemy territory, thousands of kilometres from home. Many of them died of starvation, disease and wounds. It was a rough campaign that always was on the brink of disaster .

"Yet it was miraculously successful. By 1098, the Crusaders had liberated Nicea and Antioch to Christian rule. And in July 1099 they re-conquered Jerusalem and began to rebuild a Christian state in Palestine."

A JUDGEMENT OF GOD

Crusaders rally to the Cross of Christ.

When Jerusalem fell to Saladin in 1187, Christians across Europe perceived that God was punishing them for their sins. Numerous lay movements sprang up throughout Europe dedicated to purifying Christian society so that it might become worthy of victory in the East.

Professor Madden, of St. Lewis University and the author of *A Concise History of the Crusades*, has observed: *"From the safe distance of many centuries, it is easy enough to scowl in disgust at the crusades. Religion, after all, is nothing to fight wars over. But we should be mindful that our Medieval ancestors would have been equally disgusted by our infinitely more destructive wars fought in the names of political ideologies...Whether we admire the Crusaders or not, it is a fact that the world we know today would not exist without their efforts. The ancient faith of Christianity, with its respect for women and antipathy toward slavery, not only survived but flourished. Without the crusades, it might have followed Zoroastrianism, another of Islam's rivals, into extinction.* **But for the crusades Europe would have probably fallen to Islam and the USA would never have come into existence**.

LEARN TO DISCERN

Dr. Ted Baehr of Movieguide warns viewers to be *"media wise enough to reject revisionist history"* such as the Kingdom of Heaven. *" The problem is that the future generations could accept this politically correct, anti-Christian propaganda."*

HOLLYWOOD'S CRUSADE AGAINST HISTORY

Ridley Scott's blockbuster epic **"Kingdom of Heaven"** presents one of the worst distortions of history seen on any screen in recent

Hollywood's *Kingdom of Heaven* distorts history.

years. Focusing on the fall of Jerusalem, in AD1187, to Saladin's Muslim armies, this anti-Christian, politically correct revisionism gets everything wrong.

WHO CARES ABOUT GEOGRAPHY?

First of all, Scott's *Kingdom of Heaven* has its geography very wrong. We know that the film was shot in Spain and Morocco, and it shows. Most people should know that Jerusalem is **not** in the middle of the Sahara Desert! Yet, in his film Jerusalem's high walls are surrounded by sand dunes, without a tree, a bush or a blade of grass. The Mount of Olives, the Kidron Valley and the Valley of Hinnon are nowhere to be seen. Unlike the Crusaders who liberated Jerusalem in 1099, Saladin's screen army has no problem moving his siege engines and assault towers right up to the walls of Jerusalem, because Scott's Jerusalem in *Kingdom of Heaven* is not surrounded by valleys or ditches.

This film also boldly asserts that Messina was the seaport to the Holy Land. As Messina is on the Island of Sicily, one wonders why French crusaders would, or how they could, depart from there. In fact Genoa, Venice and Naples were the ports which crusaders set sail from.

THIS IS A TRUE STORY – ONLY THE FACTS HAVE BEEN CHANGED

Kingdom of Heaven also distorts history beyond all recognition. The *"hundred-year truce"* between the Christian and Muslim armies is a figment of their imagination. The warfare throughout the 12th Century was incessant.

The depiction of the Knights Templar as a band of religious fanatics trying to shatter the truce and provoke war with the Muslims by attacking caravans, is a total fabrication. No Knights Templar ever attacked any caravans. Attacking caravans

is what the founder of Islam, Muhammad, engaged in regularly. As did his handpicked apostles, the Caliphas. The Knights Templar were formed primarily to protect travellers from the attacks of the Muslim army. In fact it was the slaughter of Christian pilgrims, by Muslim armies, in violation of earlier agreements of safe passage, that precipitated the crusades in the first place.

The central figure of this film, Sir Balian, is a historical figure, who did in fact play a critical role in the defence of Jerusalem in 1187, but the film script distorts his character and role beyond all recognition. First of all, Balian was not a blacksmith, nor did his wife commit suicide, nor was he illegitimate, nor raised as a commoner. His father, Balian the Old (not Godfrey as in the movie), had three sons, all legitimate: Hugh, Baldwin and Balian. Balian never had to travel to the Holy

Land, because he grew up as part of the nobility there. Balian was married to royalty long before the events portrayed in the film, and he was not at all romantically involved with the Princess Sybilla. (Although his brother, Baldwin, had some love interest in Sybilla).

In *Kingdom of Heaven*, Balian is portrayed as questioning whether God exists, although according to the historical records it is clear that Balian was a dedicated Christian who took his faith very seriously. Nor did Balian desert the defence of the Holy Land following the fall of Jerusalem. Far from returning to France, Balian proceeded to Beirut in Lebanon which he helped fortify against Muslim invasion. He was present with Richard the Lionhearted at the signing of the peace with Saladin, which secured safe passage for Christian pilgrims and recognised crusader control over the 90 mile stretch of coastline from Tyre to Jaffa.

According to *Kingdom of Heaven*, the real hero in the story is the famous Muslim general, Saladin (1138 – 1193). Although an exceptionally gifted military strategist and unusually chivalrous, the film has uncritically accepted, and embellished, the legends about Saladin beyond what the historical record would support. A Muslim Kurd, from Northern Iraq, Saladin was raised in a privileged family, and was very ambitious. At

In Hollywood's version, this crusader threw his helmet away just before the battle!

age 14 he joined his uncle's military staff, and at 31 followed him to Egypt where his uncle was Grand Vizier. When his uncle died two months later, Saladin seized power, defeated competing Muslim leaders and started a dynasty which established Egypt as the major Muslim power in the Middle East.

Far from having war forced upon him, Saladin

initiated the conflict by declaring a Jihad against the Christians. He swept throughout Palestine capturing more than 50 crusader castles in two years. At the battle of Hattin on 4 July 1187 Saladin's army defeated the Christians on the shores of Lake Tiberius (the Sea of Galilee) – although in the film this battle is depicted as in a waterless desert! Far from being the magnanimous victor depicted in modern legends and this film, Saladin was a ruthless general who had thousands of Christian prisoners beheaded in cold blood – including after the battle of Hattin.

In the film, Saladin is portrayed as being most gracious in allowing the defenders of Jerusalem safe passage. In fact after the negotiated surrender of Jerusalem, which the Patriarch of Jerusalem initiated, Saladin demanded that every man, woman and child in Jerusalem pay a ransom for his or her freedom or face the grim prospect of Islamic slavery. In order to save the lives and liberty of the poor people who could not afford the heavy ransom demanded by Saladin, Balian paid out of his own resources the ransom required for those who could not afford it.

TWISTED THEOLOGY

The theology in *Kingdom of Heaven* is also all wrong. The film depicts some monk standing by the roadside repeating: *"To kill an infidel is not murder it is the path to heaven!"* As any student of the Bible would be able to tell you, neither the concept nor those words appear anywhere in the Christian Bible. However, as any student of the Quran should be able to inform you, that is exactly what the Islamic doctrine of Jihad teaches.

At one point early in the film as Muslims bow in prayer towards Mecca, Balian comments: *"You allow them to pray?"* A knight sneers and answers: *"As long as they pay their taxes!"* In fact the crusaders never required any extra taxes of Muslims in order to allow them to pray. That is the Islamic doctrine and practice of *Jizya*. To this day Muslim governments require *Jizya* – tribute taxes – of *dhimmi's* (Jews and Christians under their Islamic rule).

Before the crusaders march out to the disastrous battle of Hattin, the film has one knight declaring: *"The army of Jesus Christ cannot be beaten."* However, there is no such doctrine in the Bible, or in Christian theology. It is, in fact, Islamic dogma that no Muslim army can ever be defeated by an infidel army. This Muhammad asserted on the authority of Allah himself. (Something which the recent defeats, of the Taliban, in Afghanistan, and Saddam Hussein's Muslim military superpower of the Middle East, Iraq, by the Americans has precipitated a serious theological problem for Islamic scholars).

INSULTS TO INTELLIGENCE

Quite aside from the factual errors in geography, the attributing of Islamic doctrine to the Christians, and the blatant distortion of history, the *Kingdom of Heaven* is an insult to the intelligence of its viewers in terms of its preposterous script.

Here we are expected to believe that: Balian is grieving his wife's death, yet he does not even attend to her burial; that Balian raised a commoner, trained only as a blacksmith, from France, could within days of arriving in Palestine be teaching the local people how to practise agriculture and dig wells in the desert; and that this blacksmith with no military training could know more about siege weapons and military strategy than all the knights and military professionals concentrated in the Holy Land put together! Just where would a blacksmith have learnt all about siege engines, trebuchets, cavalry tactics and defensive strategy?

The fictional, adulterous relationship depicted between Balian and Princess Sybilla strains all credibility. As does Balian's presumed ethical objection against executing the venomous and bloodthirsty husband of his presumed adulterous interest! Apparently justice and the avoiding of a disastrous war were not as important as his adulterous affections.

Aside from the terrain around Jerusalem being so conveniently flat for the invading armies, the depicted firepower and range capabilities of the catapults and trebuchets are ridiculous. Steel cranes with three-inch titanium cables would have trouble sustaining the weight and strain with which these 12th Century wooden and rope trebuchets were meant to have pulverised the thick walls of Jerusalem! The film makers of *Kingdom of Heaven* try to make up for a lack of script and character development by overdosing on computer generated explosions and fictional firepower capabilities. (Actually maximum range for a 12th Century catapult would have been 150 yards with a 300 pound rock).

The Crusaders' war machinery.

And how can any viewer with a grasp of history or military tactics swallow the kind of tactics and strategy depicted in films like *Kingdom of Heaven?* What soldiers throw their shields away just before engaging a massive assault by the enemy?! Apparently, Orlando Bloom wanted his long flowing locks to blow in the breeze, but seriously, what knight would throw his helmet away just before engaging in hand to hand combat?!

Also, as any student of history and anthropology should be able to tell you, the crusaders did not burn the bodies of their dead. That was the practice of the Vikings, the ancient Greeks and the Hindus, but not of the Christians who buried their dead.

The ridiculous speech with its feel good *"why can't we all just get along"* drivel dished up by Orlando Bloom's Balian on the walls of Jerusalem (while Saladin's armies politely delay their attack until he has finished) may sound believable to some 21st Century Humanist, but these were not the convictions or sentiments of any 12th Century crusader. As for the pathetic egalitarian gesture of knighting everybody – without any training, testing or code of conduct – is so unhistorical, and so out of touch with reality, as to make one wonder what drugs the scriptwriter was on at the time.

Then there's that shipwreck. To expect us to believe that the hero of the film could go down with the ship in high seas, and awake the next morning alive and well, on the shore – with the entire crew and every passenger, and every horse dead, and neatly deposited on the shore – is ludicrous. Especially that the only survivors of the shipwreck were the hero, and his horse! And of course, very conveniently, his father's sword was not the kind of heavy sword that would sink to the bottom of the ocean, but was also neatly deposited next to this sole survivor!

CRUSADE AGAINST CHRISTIANITY

The ridiculous and inane comments attributed to the bishop in the film are also not only highly unlikely, but jarringly anachronistic. Producer Ridley Scott, and scriptwriter William Monahan, obviously hate Christianity. But, just in case any viewers lack the discernment to detect the unveiled anti-Christian hostility and prejudice, which permeates the entire movie, Ridley Scott has gone on record as stating: *"Balian is an agnostic, just like me."* Of course there was no such thing as agnosticism in the 12th Century, especially not amongst crusaders. The word *"agnostic"* was a 19th Century invention.

Just in case anyone misunderstood the motivations behind his movie, Ridley Scott has been quoted as saying: *"If we could just take God out of the equation, there would be no f... Problem!"*

ENTERTAINMENT OR EXPLOITATION?

Considering how few people today read history books, and how most depend entirely on these kind of *"based on a true story – the names and the places are true – only the facts have been changed to protect the guilty"* films, for their understanding of the past, this kind of blind prejudice and obsessive hatred against Christianity on the part of producers and directors should be frightening. As Karl Marx declared: *"The first battlefield is the rewriting of history."* I'm sure that all the enemies of Christianity are delighted with propaganda pics like Kingdom of Heaven.

THE FACTS OF HISTORY

The fact is that the crusades of the Middle Ages were a reaction to centuries of Islamic Jihad. In the first century of Islam alone Muslim invaders conquered the whole of the previously Christian North Africa destroying over 3200 churches – in just 100 years. In the first five centuries of Islam, Muslim forces killed Christians, kidnapped their children to raise them as Muslims, or compelled people at the point of the sword to convert to Islam.

Muslim invaders lead Christian women away into slavery.

Up to 50% of all the Christians in the world were wiped out during the first three centuries of Islam. The Saracens (as the Muslim invaders were called) desecrated Christian places of worship and were severely persecuting Christians. Pilgrims were then prevented from visiting those places where our Lord was born, was crucified and raised from the dead. It was only after four centuries of Islamic Jihad that the crusades were launched as a belated reaction to the blatant Islamic Jihad.

A crusader bids farewell to his wife and child.

LOGISTICS AND ECONOMICS

As the Christian History Institute has pointed out, the characterising of crusaders as only in it for the plunder and the loot betrays an ignorance of both geography and history. The vast majority of the crusaders were impoverished and financially ruined by the crusades. Crusaders, through great sacrifice and personal expense, left their homes and families to travel 3000km across treacherous and inhospitable terrain – and the shortest crusade lasted 4 years. Considering that only 10% of the crusaders had horses, and 90% were foot soldiers, the sheer fact of logistics is that the crusaders could not possibly have carried back enough loot to have made up for the loss of earnings and high expenses involved with these long crusades. Many crusaders lost their homes and farms to finance their involvement in the crusades.

THERE'S MORE TO LIFE THAN MONEY

Perhaps self-seeking materialistic agnostics in the 21st Century cannot understand that some people could be motivated by something other than personal financial enrichment, but the fact is that many people make sacrifices for their religious convictions, and in order to help others. In the case of the crusaders, the historical record makes clear that amongst the motivations that led tens of thousands of volunteers to reclaim the Holy Land was a sense of Christian duty to help their fellow Christians in the East

Christian prisoners condemned into Islamic slavery.

whose lands had been invaded and churches desecrated by Muslim armies, and a desire to secure access to the Holy Lands for pilgrims.

There was also a desire to fight for the honour of their Lord Jesus Christ, Whose churches had been destroyed and Whose Deity had been denied by the Mohammadan aggressors. In other words, **to the crusaders this was a defensive war to reclaim Christian lands from Muslim invaders**.

We may not share their convictions, or agree with their methods, but we ought to evaluate them in the light of the realities of the 11th and 12th centuries, and not anachronistically project our standards and politics back upon them.

The Christian courage of Maille who fought to the end against an overwhelming force of Saracens.

THE MISSING JIHAD

Scriptwriter William Monahan, and Director Ridley Scott, obviously don't understand the motivations behind the crusaders, and apparently they do not understand the Islamic doctrine of *Jihad* either – which the film makes no reference to. Considering that Jihad was the central threat that had led to the reaction of the crusades, this omission is inexplicable. *Kingdom of Heaven* preoccupies itself with fictionalising crusader atrocities, but it ignores the pattern of the preceding five centuries of genocide and aggression by Islamic armies.

Scott's *Kingdom of Heaven* is politically correct, anti-Christian, pro-Muslim propaganda. It makes poor entertainment and is a worthless distortion of reality.

MUHAMMAD VS CHRIST

In his article *"Self Hate, Revisionist History and Christophobia in the movie Kingdom of Heaven"* Dr. Ted Baehr notes some of the differences between Muhammad and Christ:

- "Muhammad was the prophet of war; Christ is the Prince of Peace (Isaiah 9:6).
- Muhammad's disciples killed for the faith; Christ's disciples were killed for their faith (Acts 12:2; 2 Tim. 4:7).
- Muhammad promoted persecution against the "infidels"; Christ forgave and converted the chief persecutor (1 Tim. 1:13-15).
- Muhammad was the taker of life; Christ is the giver of life (John 10:27-28).
- Muhammad and his fellow warriors murdered thousands; Christ murdered none but saved many (John 12:48).
- Muhammad's method was COMPULSION; Christ's aim was CONVERSION (Acts 3:19).
- Muhammad practised FORCE; Christ preached FAITH (John 6:29, 35).
- Muhammad was a WARRIOR; Christ is a DELIVERER (Col. 1:13; 1 Thess. 1:10).
- Muhammad said to the masses, "Convert or die!"; Christ said, *"Believe and live!"* (John 6:47; 11:25-26).
- Muhammad was swift to shed blood (Rom. 3:15-17); Christ shed His own blood for the salvation of many (Eph. 1:7).
- Muhammad preached "Death to the infidels!"; Christ prayed *"Father, forgive them, for they know not what they do"* (Luke 23:34).
- Muhammad declared a holy war (Jihad) against infidels; Christ achieved a holy victory on Calvary's cross (Col. 2:14-15) and His followers share in that victory (John 16:33).

- Muhammad constrained people by conquest; Christ constrained people by love (2 Cor. 5:14).
- Modern terrorists derive their inspiration from Muhammad and carry out their despicable atrocities in the name of his god; Christians derive their inspiration from the One who said, *"Blessed are the peacemakers"* (Matthew 5:9).
- Modern day disciples of Muhammad respond to the terrorist attacks by cheering in the streets; modern day disciples of Christ are deeply grieved at past atrocities carried out by those who were "Christians" in name only (the Crusades, the Spanish Inquisition, etc.).
- Many Muslims are peaceful and peace-loving because they do not strictly follow the teachings of their founder; many Christians are peaceful and peace-loving because they do strictly follow the teachings of their Founder (Rom. 12:17-21).
- Muhammad called upon his servants to fight; Jesus said, "My kingdom is not of this world; if My kingdom were of this world, then would My servants fight . . . but now is My kingdom not from here" (John 18:36)
- Muhammad ordered death to the Jews (see A.Guillaume, The Life of Muhammad, Oxford University Press [1975], p. 369); Christ ordered that the Gospel be preached *"to the Jew first"* (Rom. 1:16).
- The Quran says, "Fight and slay the Pagans wherever ye find them" (Qu'ran 9.5); Christ said, *"Preach the Gospel to every creature"* (Mark 16:15).
- Muhammad's mission was to conquer the world for Allah; Christ's mission was to conquer sin's penalty and power by substitutionary atonement (2 Cor. 5:21; 1 Pet. 3:18).
- Muhammad claimed that there was but one God, Allah; Christ claimed that He was God (John 10:30-31; John 8:58-59; John 5:18; John 14:9).
- Muhammad's Tomb: OCCUPIED! Christ's tomb: EMPTY!"

JIHAD VS THE GOSPEL

The word *"crusade"* does not appear in the Bible, nor is it commanded in Christianity. However, *Jihad* is the sixth pillar of Islam and the second greatest command of Muhammad. It is not only commended, but commanded in the Quran.

The crusades ended many centuries ago, however Islamic Jihad is carried out to this day. Millions of Christians have been slaughtered throughout the centuries by Islamic militants – such as the 1.5 million Armenians murdered in Turkey in 1915. Christians have continued to be slaughtered by Islamic militants in Indonesia, the Philippines, Sudan and Nigeria to the present day.

Therefore, before Christians fall over themselves to apologise for the crusades, which ended over 700 years ago, it would be wise to first learn from reliable sources what the crusades were all about, and study the Islamic teachings and track record of Jihad over the last 14 centuries. **Those who do not know their past have no future.**

The famous Islamic oil painting of Mehemet's conquest of Constantinople depicts the Sultan's horse standing over the dead body of a Christian princess - an obviously unarmed civilian woman - with long flowing blond hair. This glorifying of a brutal massacre shows contempt for Christian women.

Chapter 16

The End of Islam

By God's grace, we are living in momentous times, which could be the beginning of the end of Islam.

Muslim states are the most severe persecutors of Christians and radical Muslim extremists are the most vicious terrorists, hijackers, kidnappers, suicide bombers and assassins in the world today.

Debris from the World Trade Centre rains down on a nearby church.

MUSLIM MYTHS

Muslims, and their public relations agents and apologists, claim that Islam is a great religion of learning and tolerance. I have heard Muslim Imams of the Islamic Propagation Centre International declare in the mosque in Durban that Muslims are *"more Jewish than the Jews and more Christian than the Christians!"* All over the world, repeatedly, Muslims claim Islam to be superior to Christianity. *"You Christians are so divided. We Muslims are all united. You have so many denominations, but we Muslims are all one. In Islam there is perfect unity."* And *"Christianity is a religion for the Whites only, Islam is the Black man's religion.";* *"There is no racism in Islam, we are all one in Islam."* *"You Christians have so many Bibles, and you keep changing the Bible, but we Muslims have only one Quran, and it has never been changed."*

JUST THE FACTS

Slavery, Terrorism and Islam exposes the falsehood of these and other prevalent myths propagated about Islam. Far from Islam being a great religion of learning, tolerance and peace, this book presents the historical facts, and sets the record straight. Muhammad declared that if other books confirmed what was in the Quran then they didn't need them. And if the books did not confirm what was in the Quran they didn't want them. So the order was: Burn them! The Muslims burned libraries all across North Africa and the Middle East. They burned the library of Alexandria - the largest library in the world at that time. It probably included original copies of the Bible and other priceless manuscripts.

A TRAIL OF DESTRUCTION

Over 3,200 churches were destroyed or converted into mosques during the first century of Islamic Jihad alone. During the Muslim invasion of Syria in AD 634 thousands of Christians were massacred. As Mesopotamia was conquered between AD 635 and 643 many churches and monasteries were ransacked, and ministers and Christians slain. In the conquest of Egypt AD 640 and 641, the towns of Behnesa, Fayum, Nikiu and Aboit were all put to the sword. When the Muslims invaded Cyprus, they looted and pillaged homes and churches and massacred much of the population. In North Africa, when Tripoli was captured in AD 643, all the Jews and Christians were forced to hand their women and children over as slaves. When Carthage was captured, it was burned to the ground and most of its inhabitants slaughtered.

Beginning in AD 712 the Muslim armies invaded India. They smashed and demolished temples, plundered palaces, slaughtered

Muslim armies conquered the whole of North Africa and Spain within the first century after Muhammad.

millions of Indian men and enslaved the women and children. The ancient cities of Baranasai Mathura, Uggain, Maheshwar, Jwalamukhi and Dwarka were sacked, the populations massacred, and not one temple left standing.

"THE BLOODIEST STORY IN HISTORY"

Will Durant in his *The Story of Civilisations*, describes the Muslim invasion of India as *"probably the bloodiest story in history."* The North Western region of India is called the Hindu Kush (*"the slaughter of the Hindu"*) as a reminder of the vast number of Hindu slaves who died while being marched across the Afghan Mountains to the Muslim slave markets in Central Asia. The Buddhists were also targeted for destruction. In AD 1193 Muhammad Khilji burned to the ground their famous library and the Buddhist stronghold of Bihar.

Shah Jahan is remembered as the builder of the Taj Mahal. What few Westerners know is that the builder of the Taj Mahal launched 48 military campaigns against non-Muslims in just 30 years. In AD 1628 he killed all his male relatives. Shah Jahan had 5,000 concubines in his harem but also indulged in incestuous sex with his daughters. In just one town, Benares, Jahan destroyed 76 Hindu temples. He also demolished Christian churches at Agra and Lahore. When he captured Hugh, a

Portuguese enclave near Calcutta, he had 10,000 inhabitants *"blown up with powder, drowned in water or burned by fire."* Another 4,000 were enslaved and offered Islam or death. Those who refused to convert were killed.

SPAIN UNDER THE MOORS

Neither was Spain, under the Muslim Moors, the jewel of Islamic tolerance that it is often purported to be. In AD 920 all the inhabitants of Muez were put to the sword. Cordova, Zarajoza and Merida were burned to the ground, with all adult males executed and all women and children enslaved. In AD 1066 all the Jews of Grenada were slaughtered. In AD 1126, all the Christians of Grenada were deported to Morocco.

In AD 1009, Kalif Hakem of Egypt ordered the destruction of the Holy Sepulchre and all Christian places of worship in Jerusalem. Christians were persecuted cruelly and pilgrims were attacked.

CARNAGE IN CONSTANTINOPLE

Under Mehemet II the Turks conquered the great Byzantine capital, Constantinople. On 29 May, AD 1453, waves of Turkish soldiers swept into Constantinople, the greatest city in the world at that time, and put

Massacre in the Hagia Sophia 28 May 1453.

it to the sword. Priceless libraries and irreplaceable works of art were burned, the population slaughtered, even in the Hagia Sophia, the greatest Christian church in the world at that time.

For centuries the Turks demanded an annual "blood levy" of Christian boys. Parents were forced to hand over one out of every five Christian boys for service in the Sultan's army as janissaries.

THE FORGOTTEN HOLOCAUSTS

Slavery, Terrorism and Islam documents hundreds of massacres of Christian populations by Muslim rulers. For example: In 1860 over 12,000 Christians were slaughtered in Lebanon. In 1876 14,700 Bulgarians were murdered by the Turks. 200,000 Armenian Christians were slaughtered by the Turks in Bayazid in 1877. And in 1915 the Turks massacred over 1.5 million Armenian

A massacre of Armenian Christians in Turkey.

Christians. As recently as September 1922 the Turkish army destroyed the ancient city of Smyrna with its 300,000 Christian population.

INTOLERANT AND INCONSISTENT

Despite Islam proclaiming itself as a religion of tolerance, no Muslim countries allow freedom of religion. Despite the Saudi Arabian government funding the building of thousands of mosques in

Another massacre of Christians by the Turks.

Christian lands, no church or synagogue is tolerated in Saudi Arabia. Nor can any Saudi Arabian citizen be a Christian. Despite Muhammad being called a "prophet of peace", he engaged in 47 battles and raids on caravans in his lifetime. It is inconsistent of Islam to insist on the cutting off of the hand of a thief when Muhammad and his successors, the Caliphas, engaged in wholesale theft, raiding caravans, kidnapping hostages for ransom and looting homes.

INTELLECTUAL DISHONESTY

The persecution of Christians by Muslims has become a taboo subject in Western circles. Over thirteen centuries of religious discrimination

and persecution, causing the suffering, oppression, murder and enslavement of countless millions has been buried under a thick whitewash of myths of "Islamic tolerance". The deceit, cowardice and silence of all too many Western journalists and academics continues to facilitate the religious

A Muslim mob screams for the blood of Christians.

discrimination and persecutions of radical Muslims to this day.

The intellectual dishonesty of those Westerners who engage in academic gymnastics to justify the invasion of other people's lands; the looting, pillaging, raping, murdering and enslaving of whole peoples, needs to be exposed. The hypocrisy of those who justify the military aggression of Muslims, but condemn those who inflicted defeats upon these Muslim invaders needs to be challenged. The fiction that *"Jihad has never been an aggressive, but only a defensive concept"*, should be dismissed with the contempt that such deception deserves. What were Saudi Arabians defending in Spain?

DOUBLE TALK

When Islam defines a refusal to submit to Sharia law under Islam as aggression, and when they define peace as submission to Islam, then we must know that we are not talking the same language.

The long line that led to death - deportation of Christians from their homes in Armenia in 1915.

In the USA, at various airport chapels, I've noticed the increasing practice of providing prayer mats and qiblahs to indicate the direction Muslims must face to pray towards Mecca. Qurans and quantities of glossy publications printed by the Saudi Arabian Embassy to promote Islam overflow the tables at these chapels.

Even at Epcot Centre in Disney World, in their Progress Through The Ages, there is a section praising the religion of Islam, which *"kept learning alive"* during the Dark Ages! Perhaps burning libraries provided some light, but the destruction of millions of books is hardly the way to *"keep learning alive!"*

Numerous films from Hollywood have portrayed Christians as benighted, closed-minded bigots and the Muslim characters as compassionate, intelligent and enlightened. There has been a relentless barrage of anti-Christian bias and pro-Islamic propaganda generated by Hollywood

A picture of Christian Armenians lined up and shot in cold blood by the Turks.

filmmakers, liberal journalists and college professors. As Karl Marx declared: *"The first battlefield is the rewriting of history!"*

Turkish soldiers pose with the decapitated heads of Christian Armenians.

DIVISIONS AND DISSENSION

Despite Muslim claims to the contrary, the unity of Muslims is more of a thin veneer than a reality. Muslims are divided into three mega blocks: The Sunni *("one of the path")*, the Shi'ites (those who believe that Muhammad's son-in-law Ali was the true successor to Muhammad), and the Sufi (the mystical sect of Islam). These three main blocks can be broken down into literally thousands of identifiable groupings with major variations and distinctives.

One of the more obvious evidences of the divisions within Islam are the many wars waged

This winning exhibit of an Islamic sand castle competition is of an aircraft crashing into a building.

between Muslims. Since the *"Wars of Apostasy"* (that raged during the Caliph Abu Bakr's brief rule following the death of Muhammad) to more recent years, the Muslim world has been torn by revolutions and assassinations. Just since 1948, the 21 Arab countries have suffered 30 wars, 63 successful revolutions, at least 75 unsuccessful revolutions and the murder of 36 Heads of State.

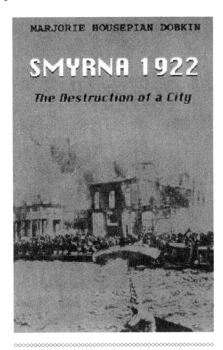

In the Arab world, revolutions and assassinations have been the most prevalent means of political expression and of attaining power. The only Arab country that was ever a democracy was Lebanon, when Christians were the majority there. However, after the Syrian invasion and intensified persecution of Christians led many to flee, and the Muslims to gain the majority, democracy in Lebanon was extinguished.

CHANGES IN THE QURAN

As to the myth that *"there is only one Quran and it has never been changed"*, Slavery, Terrorism and Islam exposes that as falsehood as well. Both the times of prayer and the direction of prayer were changed from the original Quran. Originally Muhammad had declared that it was Allah's will that all Muslims pray towards Jerusalem. After the Jews refused to accept his *"prophethood"*, Muhammad changed the direction of prayer from Jerusalem to Mecca.

DESTROYING QURANS

The third Calipha Uthman forcibly standardised the many variations of the Quran by demanding that all versions and copies of the Quran

Shi'ite Muslims demonstrate their devotion by cutting themselves with swords.

had to be surrendered - under pain of death - for destruction. At the end, Uthman issued a new, revised, standardised, version of the Quran which endures to this day.

A Muslim mother encourages her son to cut himself with a sword.

MANY VERSIONS

As to there being only one version of the Quran, I have on my shelf a number of Qurans, several of which I obtained from the Islamic Propagation Centre International, including the translation and commentary by Yusuf Ali and the translation by Muhammad Pickthall. There are also the translations by Maulana

Muhammad Ali, Ahmed Ali, J. M. Rodwell, A. J. Arberry, M. H. Shakir, N. J. Dawood and Muhammad Zafulla Khan. The differences between these various translations of the Quran can be quite interesting. For example the permitting of plunder in Surah 24:29: Rodwell translates it as *"there shall be no harm in your entering (unoccupied) houses…for the supply of your needs"*; M. Z. Khan's translation adds *"wherein are your goods."* Dawood inserts *"to seek shelter."* M. H. Shakir and M. M. Ali insert an ambiguous *"wherein you have your necessities."* Ahmed Ali writes *"where there is some convenience for you."* Whereas Arberry has a vague *"wherein enjoyment is for you."*

Shi'ite Muslims demonstrate their commitment with bloodletting.

Surah 4:34 (or:38, some versions of the Quran vary slightly as to their verse numbers), Dawood, Arberry and Rodwell translate as *"as for (disobedient wives) beat them"* whereas M. M. Ali and M. Z. Khan prefer a more obscure translation: *"chastise them."*

Some Muslim translators such as M. M. Ali tried to soften Muhammad's savagery by retranslating verses such as Surah 8:12: *"Strike off their heads. Strike off their fingertips!"* with *"smite…their necks…and every fingertip."*

Dawood translates Surah 8:68: *"A prophet may not take captives until he has fought and triumphed in the land."* However, Rodwell uses these words in his translation: *"…until he has made a slaughter in the earth."* Plainly the assertion that there is only one Quran, and the Quran has never been changed, is false.

ISLAMIC RACISM

Similarly, the claim that *"there is no racism in Islam, we are all one…"* is a blatant lie. From the very inception of Islam, and for its entire history,

The late founder of the Islamic Propagation Centre International, Ahmed Deedat.

Muslims have made up the largest numbers of slave traders and engaged in the greatest slave trading campaigns in history. Even today, slavery continues in many parts of the Muslim world. Just about the only places in the world today where you will still find slavery practised are in the Muslim world.

Muhammad was a slave owner, and he traded in slaves. Throughout the Hadith, Black people are referred to as slaves. In fact, in the Arabic language it is impossible to distinguish between a Black person and a slave. The same word used for a slave is the word for a Black man. In the Hadith Muhammad is quoted as referring to Black people as *"raisin heads."*

Several years ago when I was having a debate with Ahmed Deedat at the Islamic Propagation Centre International in Durban, Deedat tried to change the subject to get out of a sticky corner he had painted

The assassination of Egyptian president Sadat.

himself into by some theological gymnastics. *"Kafirs!"* Deedat shouted *"that's what the White Christians called the Black people when they came here to South Africa: Kafirs! That's what the Whites called the Black people: Kafirs!"* For some time Deedat continued to try to shout this refrain and change the subject, injecting some kind of racial animosity in the mixed group which was listening to this debate.

So I asked him the question: *"But isn't 'Kafir' an Arabic word? From the Quran? Isn't 'Kafir' the Arabic word for infidel? Wasn't it the Muslim slave traders who gave the people of Africa the term 'Kafirs?'"* Ahmed Deedat promptly changed the subject and never answered the question. Nor did he revisit the issue.

THE ISLAMIC SLAVE TRADE

As Slavery, Terrorism and Islam documents, at least 28 million Africans were enslaved in the Muslim Middle East. As at least 80% of those captured by Muslim slaver raiders were calculated to have died before reaching the slave markets, it is estimated that the death toll from the 14 centuries of Muslim slave raids into Africa could have been over 112 million. When added to the number of those sold in the slave markets, the total number of African victims of the Trans Sahara and East African slave trade could be significantly higher than 140 million people.

Victims of the Islamic slave trade in Africa.

There were many children born to slaves in the Americas, and millions of their descendants are citizens in Brazil and the USA to this day, but very few descendants of the slaves that ended up in the Middle East survive. Most of the male slaves destined for the Middle East slave bazaars were castrated and most of the children born to the women were killed at birth - in order to maintain Arab numerical supremacy.

CHRISTIAN ROOTS IN AFRICA

As to the Muslim claim that *"Christianity is a religion for the Whites only, Islam is the Black mans' religion."* African Christians point out that Christianity predated Islam in Africa by 6 centuries. St. Mark, the author of the Gospel of Mark, planted the Church in Egypt, in AD 62, and died for Christ in Alexandria. The Apostle Matthew, author of Matthew's Gospel, planted the Church in Abyssinia, (present day Ethiopia). Acts chapter 8 records the baptism of the treasurer of Queen Candice of Sudan, by the deacon Phillip. From the 1st Century the Church was firmly established in Egypt, Sudan and Abyssinia. Christianity came to Africa before it even went to Europe. It was an African, Simon of Cyrene, who helped carry the cross of Christ. Some of the greatest names in early Church history were Africans, including St. Augustine of Hippo, Clement of Alexandria, Tertullian, Origen and Athanasius.

AFRICA'S AGONY

However, the Muslim armies wiped out the indigenous African Church that flourished in the countries which became Libya, Tunisia, Algeria and Morocco. Through the centuries the Christians in Egypt, Sudan and Abyssinia steadfastly resisted centuries of Islamic Jihad and persecution. Far from Islam being the Black man's religion, it has been the greatest affliction the Black people have ever endured through the 14 centuries of Islamic slave trade and the oppression of Sharia law.

Today, despite Muslims being only one sixth of the world's population, Muslim armies and terrorist groups are involved in 90% of the world's conflicts.

CULTURAL DISASTER

It is no wonder that William Muir (1819 - 1905) one of the greatest orientalists of all time, concluded at the end of his long and distinguished career: *"The sword of Muhammad and the Quran are the most fatal enemies of civilisation, liberty and truth which the world has ever known...an unmitigated cultural disaster parading as God's will..."*

To this, many journalists and professors will claim that Islam was tremendously advanced scientifically and medically, while Europe languished in the Dark Ages. However, as French historian Ernest Renan observed: *"Science and philosophy flourished during the first half of the Middle Ages, but it was not by reason of Islam; it was in spite of Islam. Not a...philosopher or scholar escaped persecution...To give Islam the credit for... so many illustrious thinkers who passed half their life in prison, in forced hiding, in disgrace, whose books were burned and whose writings were suppressed by their theological authority, is as if one were to ascribe to the inquisition...a whole scientific development which it tried to prevent."*

PLUNDERING PROGRESS

What most of these propagandists for Islam choose to forget is that the Arab armies conquered the advanced Christian civilisations in North Africa and the Middle East. So, yes, by reason of plunder and occupation, the Islamic

Christian slaves of Muslims in North Africa.

Empire was enriched and benefited immeasurably. But almost all of the scientific and technological advancements, and almost all of the hard work, were the work of Christian slaves and dhimmis.

Faced as we are by the massive block of Islamic nations, and the vast petro-dollar funding of Islamic Propagation Centres, with their building of thousands of mosques and madrasses throughout Europe, Africa and the Americas, what hope is there for the future?

9-11

First of all, the Scripture is clear: ***"The desert tribes will bow before Him and His enemies will lick the dust...all kings will bow down to Him and all nations will serve Him."*** Psalm 72:9-11

That's the 9/11 of the Scriptures. Probably the most foolish thing Muslim radicals have ever done was attacking the financial heart of America with the terror attacks on the New York World Trade Centre and Washington with hijacked aircraft. Since September the 11th 2001, more critical books on Islam have been written than in previous centuries. And we have begun to see the first cracks in the monolithic empire of Islam.

TYRANTS OVERTHROWN

The Taliban, probably the most radical Islamic regime in the world,

The largest mosque in the Southern Hemisphere - in Durban.

in Afghanistan, was toppled by US forces. For the first time free elections have been held in Afghanistan. Then Saddam Hussein's regime in Iraq, the military superpower of the Muslim world was defeated by the American and Allied forces in a matter of weeks. (The Americans also organised the first free elections in Iraq's history).

Also, in the first free elections in Nigerian history, a Christian president came to power. For 38 years Nigeria suffered under a succession of Islamic dictators. Nigeria hosted the Islam in Africa Conference and was recognised as an officially Islamic state by the World Islamic Organisation. Although Sharia law continues to be enforced in the 12 Northern provinces of Nigeria, with hundreds of churches having been burned, and thousands of Christians massacred, the population of Nigeria has plainly rejected Islamic rule and a Christian president was in power there for the first time.

MORE DEFEATS FOR ISLAM

Next the National Islamic Front Government of Sudan which had waged Jihad against the Christian Black South, seeking to impose its policies of Islamisation and Arabisation, have now agreed to a cease-fire and signed a peace treaty. This peace treaty grants autonomy to the South, exempting them from Sharia law and recognising some religious freedom. Then Malawi, which had for ten years been ruled by a Muslim president, elected a Christian president.

SHAKING FOUNDATIONS

In 2005 *The Passion of the Christ* film was shown throughout the Muslim world to overflowing theatres. Never before had any Christian medium impacted the lives of tens of millions of Muslims. Missionaries in the Middle East rejoiced that more people had seen *The Passion* in a single day in their city than they had been able to show the Jesus film in the previous four years of full-time missionary work! While the *Jesus* film was illegal and could only be shown secretly, at great risk, *The Passion* was being openly screened in the shopping mall cinemas! This, taken along with the phenomenal response to SAT-7, a Christian mission broadcasting Gospel programmes in Arabic throughout the Middle East, is also unprecedented.

Then we should mention the Cedar Revolution in Lebanon, and Libya's sudden renouncing of terrorism and seeking to co-operate with the USA. Taken together with the facts that: there are more missionaries

The King of France with King Richard the Lionhearted, of England, on the Third Crusade.

focused on the Muslim world today than ever before in history, more books written on Islam from a Christian perspective than ever before, and there is also more prayer focused on the Muslim world than ever before. All of these factors considered together represent a series of seismic events shaking the very foundations of Islam.

THE THREAT OF FREEDOM

Islam cannot survive freedom. The Quran cannot survive intense scrutiny and critical investigation. In this technological age, Islam's days are numbered. Although they can hijack Western technology to use against the West, the foundations of Islam are rotten to the core and cannot stand.

The Scriptures declare: *"At the Name of Jesus every knee will bow...every tongue confess that Jesus Christ is Lord..."* Philippians 2:10-11.

The day will come when the earth will be as full of the knowledge of the glory of the Lord as the seas are full of water (Habakkuk 2:14).

Yet it is also true that *"My people are destroyed from lack of knowledge"* (Hosea 4:6). There is a tremendous ignorance of Islam and most Christians are failing to evangelise their Muslim neighbours. That is why this book, *Slavery, Terrorism and Islam* is needed at this time. We need to understand Islam and we need to evangelise Muslims.

> *"The harvest is plentiful, but the workers are few. Ask the Lord of the harvest therefore to send out workers into His harvest field."*   Matthew 9:39

Pray for the persecuted Christians suffering under Islam. Pray for the women suffering under Islam. And pray that the Church may respond to the threat of Islam with prayer and action - to win Muslims for Christ.

> *"Go, therefore, and make disciples of all nations..."*   Matthew 28:19

General Charles Gordon bravely faced the Mahdi's forces in the siege of Khartoum, 1885. As Governor of the Sudan, Gordon had abolished slavery and effectively erradicated the slave trade. In reaction the Mahdi mobilised an uprising to re-establish slavery in Sudan. General Gordon was beheaded and the entire population of Khartoum put to the sword by the Mahdi's Dervishes.

Glossary of Islamic Terms

A.H.	(*After Hijrah*) abbreviation for the Muslim calendar; used to divide time, counting from the flight of Muhammad to Medina (in AD 622).
Adhan	The daily call to prayer by the muezzin from the mosque.
Affliction	The existence of people who are non-Muslims.
Ahl-al-Kitab	*"The people of the Book"* (that is: Christians).
Allah'u-Akbar	*"Allah is great"*.
Al Mesih	The Messiah.
Assalaam Alykum	*"Peace be upon you"*, used as a greeting.
Ayatollah	Literally a *"sign of Allah"*; a term of honour for a religious leader of Shi'ite Islam.
Bani-e-Islam	The founder of Islam (Muhammad).
Banu	tribe
Bint	daughter
Calipha	A successor to Muhammad, a Vice-Regent, the spiritual and political leader of the whole Muslim community worldwide (Also spelt Khalifah).
Dar-al-Harb	The House of War - all those nations not yet under sharia law.
Dar-al-Islam	The House of Peace - those nations in complete subjection to sharia law

Da'wah	The missionary movement of Islam in the sense of making converts and spreading Islam.
Dhimmi	Non-Muslims in an Islamic society, subjugated as second class citizens under Islamic control.
Din (Deen)	Way of religion, way of life, duties in Islam, such as reciting the creed, praying, fasting and giving alms.
Eid	Feast day or celebration.
Fatwa	A ruling in Islamic law.
Hadith	The collection of traditions about the life of Muhammad.
Hafiz	A person who can memorise the whole Quran.
Hajj	Pilgrimage to Mecca - one of the pillars of Islam.
Halaal	Something lawful or permitted, as in Halaal food.
Haraam	Something which is forbidden, or not allowed, in Islam.
Hijrah	Muhammad's flight to Medina, AD 622.
Houris	The beautiful, fair skinned maidens, with almond shaped eyes who delight *"the faithful"* in paradise.
Ibn	Son
Imam	The leader who guides the prayers in the mosque.
Insha'lhah	*"If Allah wills."*
Isa	Arabic name for Jesus.
Islam	Submission, surrender or subjugation.
Jihad	Holy War, the sixth pillar of Islam, and according to Muhammad, the second most important deed in Islam.

Jinn	Spirits
Jizya	Tribute taxes required of dhimmi's - Christians and Jews under Islamic rule.
Jumma	Friday, the Muslim holy day.
Ka'ba	Cube shaped building in Mecca towards which all Muslims must bow in prayer. On its Eastern corner a black stone *("come from heaven")* a meteorite is located. The Ka'ba was used as a shrine for idol worship in pre-Islamic times.
Kafir	An infidel, an unbeliever.
Kalima	Islamic creed: *"There is no God but Allah and Muhammad is his prophet."*
Kalimatu'llah	*"The Word of God"* - Jesus, the Messiah.
Khutbah	Sermon or speech at the mosque on Fridays.
Kitab	Book
Kitabi	One of the *"People of the Book"*.
Madressa	Islamic school.
Mahdi	*"The guided one"*, a Muslim military messiah expected by the Shi'ites to return at the end of time.
Martyr	One who dies whilst trying to kill infidels.
Masjid	House of worship or mosque.
Mecca	The birthplace of Muhammad in Saudi Arabia, it must be visited by all Muslims in pilgrimage at least once in their lifetime.
Medina	The second most holy city of Islam to which Muhammad fled in AD 622.

Mihrab	The niche in a mosque indicating the direction of prayer (Qibla).
Mimbar	Pulpit in mosque.
Minaret	The tower of a mosque to call people to prayer.
Miraj	The supposed night journey of Muhammad to the temple in Jerusalem and then up to the seventh heaven.
Mishkat	The collection of *"most authentic"* Sunni traditions.
Muezzin	A person who does the call to prayer five times a day from the mosque.
Mujahid	A warrior in Jihad.
Mullah	A teacher of Islam.
Murtadd	An apostate of Islam.
Muslim	*"One who submits,"* a follower of Muhammad.
Nabi	Prophet
Oppression	Refusal to submit to Islam.
Quran (or Koran)	*"The Reading"* or *"Reciting"*. Believed by Muslims to be the word of Allah revealed to Muhammad by the Angel Gabriel over a 23 year period.
Qiblah	The direction Muslims must face when they pray towards Mecca.
Ramadan	The ninth month in the Islamic calendar the month for fasting from sunrise to sunset.
Salaam	*Peace The enforcement of Sharia law. The absence of resistance to Islam.*

Salat The prescribed five daily prayers. One of the pillars of Islam. A Muslim who neglects these prayers is regarded as an apostate and must be killed if he does not repent.

Sawn The act of fasting.

Shaháda *"To bear witness"* which is done by reciting the creed.

Shari'a Islamic law based on the Quran and the Hadith.

Shi'ites The sect of Islam that believes that Muhammad's son-in-law Ali was the true successor to Muhammad.

Shirk Associating anyone with Allah as a co-deity. The worst sin in Islam.

Strive Fight

Sufi Mystical sect of Islam.

Sunni *"One of the path,"* main group of Muslims.

Surah *"A row"* or *"series"* used exclusively for chapters in the Quran (There are 114 chapters in the Quran).

Talaq A word used by a husband to divorce his wife.

Tasbih A rosary of 99 beads used for prayer.

Taurat The Law of Moses, the first five books of the Old Testament.

Umma The people of Islam, the whole community of Islam worldwide.

Zakat A religious offering. A devout Muslim is supposed to give one fortieth (2,5%) of his income, primarily to the poor and needy.

Zabur The Psalms of David.

Appendix II

Who's Who in Islam

Abdu'llah	Father of Muhammad; *"a slave of Allah"*.
Abdu'l-Muttalib	Grandfather of Muhammad; his first guardian.
Abdul Cassim	The proper name of Muhammad.
Abu Talib	Uncle and guardian of Muhammad.
Ahmad	*"Praised one"*; same word root as Muhammad.
Al-Baizawi	Commentator (900 AH).
Al-Baqawi	(or al-Baghawi) Commentator (515 AH).
Al-Bukhari	Collector of traditions about Muhammad (AD 810-871).
Al-Ghazzali	Islamic teacher (450 AH).
Allah	(from al-illah); apparently the chief deity in pre-Islamic Mecca; later the one god of Islam.
Amina	Mother of Muhammad.
Dawood	King David.
Fatima	The daughter of Muhammad, who had an offspring through Ali.
Ibrahim	Abraham.
Isa	Name used in the Quran for Jesus.
Jibril	Angel Gabriel.
Moosa (or Musa)	Moses.

Muhammad	(or Mohammed) the prophet of Islam (*"the praised one"*).
Quraish	Arab tribe from which Muhammad originated and from which all Caliphs were to be chosen.
Suleiman	Soloman.
Yahya	John the Baptist.
Zaid-ibn-Harith	Muhammad's adopted son, whose divorced wife Zainab he later married.
Zaid-ibn-Thabit	Compiler of the Quran (14 AH).

THE FIRST FOUR CALIPHAS

Abu-Bakr	Rich and respected merchant of Mecca. One of the first converts of Islam. A close follower of Muhammad and first Calipha (AD 632-634). He was also Muhammad's father-in-law (through Ayesha).
Umar	Second Calipha (AD 634-644). He was assassinated while in prayer.
Uthman	Third Calipha (AD 644-656). He ordered the editing of the Quran. Thereafter all documents were destroyed to preserve the unity of the text. He was murdered.
Ali	Nephew and adopted son of Muhammad, who married Fatima and became the fourth Calipha. He was murdered.

WIVES OF MUHAMMAD (Those whose names we know)

Khadijah Bint Khuwalid

Sa'uda Bint Zama

Ayesha Bint Abu Bakr

Hafsah Bint Umar

Zainab Bint Khusaima

Umm Salama

Zainab Bint Jahsh

Juwairiyya Bint Al-Harith

Safiyah Bint Huyai Akhtab

Umm Habiba

Maimunah Bint Al-Harith

SLAVE CONCUBINES OF MUHAMMAD

Rihana (The Jewess)

Miryam (Mary the Copt)

Jameelah

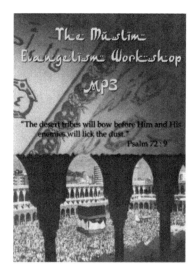

Proselytizing to Peace - Jihad in Action

Appendix III

Violence Level

Muslim Population

Country Examples

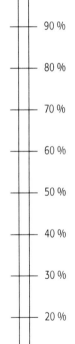

Peace
- "Dar-Es-Salaam" (House of Peace)

100 %

Saudi Arabia, Libya, Yemen

Genocide
- State-run ethnic cleansing

90 %

Turkey - Armenia

Baha'i Minority, Iran
Northern Nigeria

80 %

Persecution
- Sporadic ethnic cleansing
- Sharia law as a weapon
- Jizya tax, confiscations
- Expulsions (emigration)

70 %

Biafra

Sudan
Kosovo
Lebanon

Massacres
- Chronic terror attacks
- Green-lines
- Massacres
- On-going militia warfare

60 %

Egypt
Bosnia

50 %

Southern Nigeria
Western Papua New Guinea

East Timor

Rioting
- Hair-trigger rioting
- Jihadi militia formation
- Sporadic killings
- Church bombing

40 %

Moluccas

30 %

Israel
India
Mindinao

Belligerence
- Over represented in jails
- No-go, lawless suburbs
- Grievance fabrication
- Statements of identity

20 %

France
Holland
Germany
USA

Proselytising
- From ethnic minorities, predators,
  & the disaffected

10 %

Australia
South Africa
Japan

0 %

Adapted from a chart in *Jihad*

The Spread of Islam
According to Islamic Sources

Appendix IV

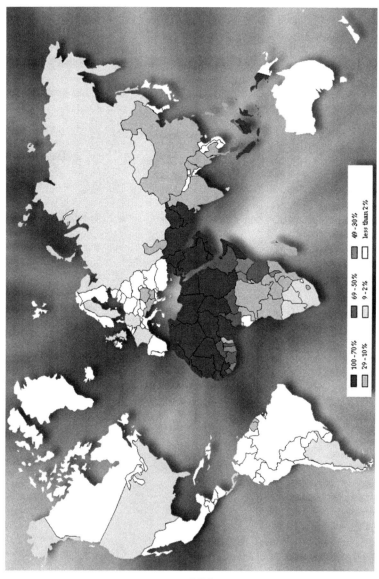

Source: www.islamicweb.com

Percentage of Muslims by Country

Appendix V

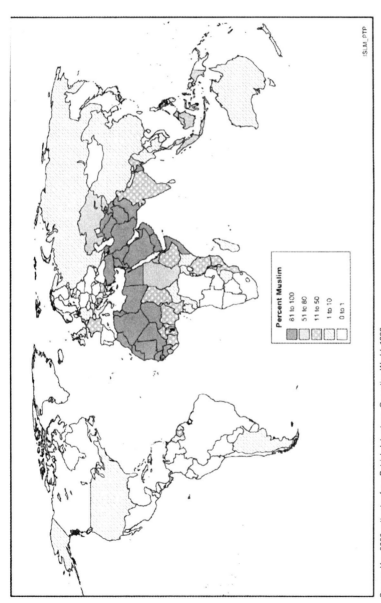

Source: Year 2000 estimates from Patrick Johnstone, Operation World, 1993.
Note: Western Sahara religion figures reflect Morocco religion totals.
Produced by Global Mapping International, 3/00. (719) 531-3599

Population Density of Muslims

Appendix VI

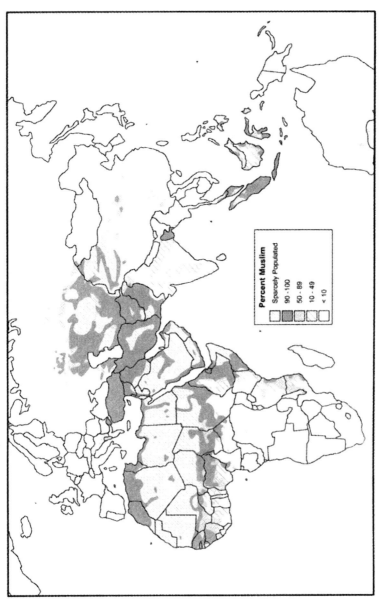

Source: Based on "A Map of the Muslims in the World".
A map from the center for Advanced Studies on Modern Asia and Africa, 1984.
Produced by Global Mapping International, 3/00. (719) 531-3599

Muslim Population by Country

Appendix VII

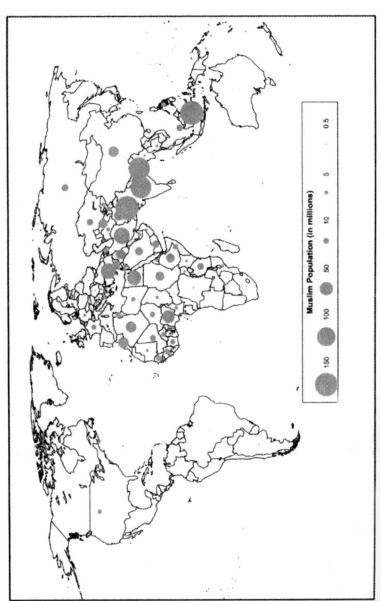

Note: Western Sahara Muslim figures reflected in Morocco totals.
Dot in each country is proportionally sized to the estimated number of Muslims in that country.
Source: Year 2000 estimates from Patrick Johnstone, Operation World, 1993.
Produced by Global Mapping International, 3/00. (719) 531-3599

Muslim Growth Rate

Appendix VIII

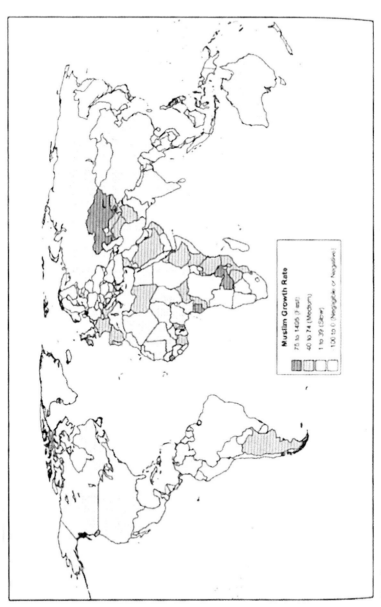

Note: Percent growth rate over 10 year period, 1990-2000.
Countries less than .1 percent Muslim have been included in the Negligible category.
Derived from 1990-2000 religion growth figures. Patrick Johnstone, Operation World, 1993
Produced by Global Mapping International, 3/00. (719) 531-3599

Military Spending and National Prosperity

Appendix IX

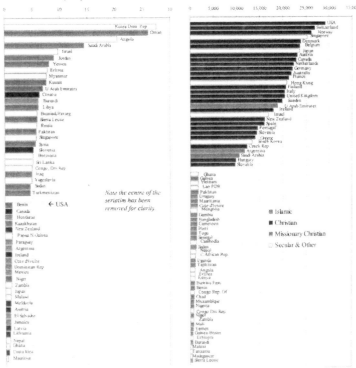

Military Spending
Spending as % of GDP

National Prosperity
GDP/Capita in $US

Note the centre of the seriatim has been removed for clarity.

← USA

- Islamic
- Christian
- Missionary Christian
- Secular & Other

Prosperity and Corruption

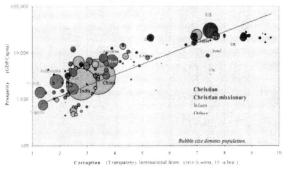

Prosperity (GDP/Capita)

Christian
Christian missionary
Islam
Other

Bubble size denotes population.

Corruption (Transparency International Score. rate is worst, 10 is best.)

Appendix X

Churchill on Islam

Winston Leonard Spencer Churchill was one of the pre-eminent figures of the 20th Century. He was awarded the Nobel Prize for Literature in 1953.

Churchill gained first-hand knowledge of Islam in the army. In 1895, he was posted in the North-West Frontier of India (now Pakistan), bordering Afghanistan.

He wrote in *The Story of the Malakand Field Force*: *"Indeed it is evident that Christianity must always exert a modifying influence on men's passions, and protect them*

from the more violent forms of fanatical fever. But the Mohammedan religion increases, instead of lessening, the fury of intolerance. It was originally propagated by the sword, and forever since, its votaries have been subject, above the people of all other creeds, to this form of madness."

"Civilisation is confronted with militant Mohammedanism. The forces of progress clash with those of reaction. The religion of blood and war is face to face with that of peace. Luckily the religion of peace is usually the better armed."

He also joined Lord Kitchener's army in the Sudan, and took part in the Battle of Omdurman on September 2, 1898.

Churchill wrote *The River War: An account of the Reconquest of Sudan:* "*How dreadful are the curses which Mohammedanism lays on it's votaries! Besides the fanatical frenzy, which is as dangerous in a man as hydrophobia in a dog, there is this fearful fatalistic apathy. Improvident habits, slovenly systems of agriculture, sluggish methods of commerce, and insecurity of property exist wherever the followers of the Prophet rule or live. A degraded sensualism deprives this life of its grace and refinement; the next of its dignity and sanctity. The fact that in Mohammedan law every woman must belong to some man as his absolute property either as a child, a wife, or a concubine must delay the final extinction of slavery until the faith of Islam has ceased to be a great power among men.*

"*Individual Moslems may show splendid qualities. Thousands become the brave and loyal soldiers of the Queen: all know how to die. But the influence of their religion paralyses the social development of those who follow it. No stronger retrograde force exists in the world. Far from being moribund, Mohammedanism is a militant and proselytizing faith. It has already spread throughout Central Africa, raising fearless warriors at every step; and were it not that Christianity is sheltered in the strong arms of science - the science against which it had vainly struggled - the civilisation of modern Europe might fall, as fell the civilisation of ancient Rome.*

"*What the horn is to the rhinoceros, what the sting is to the wasp, the Mohammedan faith is to the Arabs of the Sudan - a faculty of offence.*

"*All the warlike operations of Mohammedan peoples are characterised by fanaticism. The Mahdi became the absolute master of the Sudan. Whatever pleasures he desired he could command, and, following the example of the founder of the Mohammedan faith, he indulged in what would seem to Western minds gross excesses. He established an extensive harem for his own peculiar use, and immured therein the fairest captives of the war."*

Churchill noted the threat of Wahhabism on June 14, 1921 at the House of Commons. At that time, Churchill was Secretary for the British colonies, and he had been involved in the formation of Iraq (in 1921), Jordan (Transjordan) and Palestine, territories which Britain had liberated from the Ottoman (Turkish) Empire.

A large number of Bin Saud's followers belong to the Wahabi sect, a form of Mohammedanism. *"The Wahhabis profess a life of exceeding austerity, and what they practice themselves they rigorously enforce on others. They hold it as an article of duty, as well as of faith, to kill all who do not share their opinions and to make slaves of their wives and children. Women have been put to death in Wahhabi villages for simply appearing on the streets.*

"Austere, intolerant, well-armed, and blood-thirsty, in their own regions the Wahhabis are a distinct factor which must be taken into account, and they have been, and still are, very dangerous to the holy cities of Mecca and Medina."

The Bin Saud to whom Churchill refers here is King Abdul Aziz bin Saud (c. 1880-1953), who would go on officially to establish Saudi Arabia in 1932. The Wahhabists slaughtered 25 of the Mahmal caravan members at Mina because they played trumpets. Music was forbidden to the Wahhabists. The incident soured relations between Egypt and Saudi Arabia.

Churchill said: *"An appeaser is one who feeds the crocodile hoping it will eat him last. Victory will never be found by taking the line of least resistance."*

Appendix XI

Death Threats from Mulsim Extremists

Monday, 18 July 2005, the Frontline Fellowship Field Director was surrounded by a mob of Muslim students at the University of Pretoria threatening him and demanding that the Frontline Fellowship missions display be removed. We had been officially invited by the University Missions Committee to take part in their *"Go Love the Nations"* Missions Week.

MUSLIM MOB AT MISSIONS WEEK

Within two hours of setting up the Frontline Fellowship missions display. We began to receive hostile reactions from Muslim students, some of whom swore and cursed at our missionary, and threatened his life. Soon a mob of fifteen to twenty Muslim students were surrounding the Frontline mission display shouting and swearing at him. Some tore up or burned Frontline literature. A Muslim member of the Student Representative Council then fetched the Dean of students to inform us that we had to dismantle the Frontline mission display, and return later that afternoon when things had calmed down.

That afternoon, we were informed by the TUKS Missions Committee that they could not allow our mission display to be set up again. It was mentioned that the Frontline Fellowship newsletters, in what they reported on the activities and teachings of Muslims, were too offensive to the Muslim students.

HOSTILE PHONE CALLS

On the same day, our mission in Cape Town received a number

of hostile phone calls from Muslims. The two phone calls that I personally dealt with were with people who identified themselves as Muslim students of the University of Pretoria. The first was from a Muslim woman who was quite abusive and emotional, swearing and threatening me. When I asked for any specific factual inaccuracies in our publications she preferred to curse me and threaten retribution for having *"insulted the prophet Muhammad"*. She asked how dare we come to what she termed *"our university"*. When I asked which university that was, she reiterated *"Pretoria University, our university"*. I asked whether universities were not meant to be places of free speech. Her answer made clear that she believed that freedom of speech should only be for Islam, not Christianity.

When I asked her if she, as a woman, would be free to drive a motorcar in Saudi Arabia, or whether she would have the vote in Saudi Arabia, she became particularly emotional and abusive, and asked *"what the hell does that have to do with you? Saudi Arabia is our country! It's none of your business what we do in our country!"* When I asked how Pretoria University could be *"her"* university and Saudi Arabia be her home at the same time, she slammed the phone down.

The second caller was more controlled, but also threatened serious consequences and hell fire for having *"insulted the prophet Muhammad"*. I made clear that if there were any factual errors in our publications, we would be keen to rectify that. He didn't mention any specific inaccuracies in our **End of Islam** article, but only that it was *"insulting to the prophet Muhammad"*. He defended the fact that there were no churches or missionaries allowed in Saudi Arabia, because it is a Muslim country. When I asked how then he could object to a Christian mission having a display at a Christian Missions Week in the University of Pretoria, he reiterated that Pretoria is *"our University"* and we were not welcome there.

DEATH THREAT FATWA BY FAX

These abusive phone calls, coming along with a death threat *fatwa*, which I had received the previous week, and a Muslim mob intimidating a Students Mission Committee to expel a mission to Muslims from the university Missions Week, had ominous implications.

The death threat informed me that as the Director of Frontline Fellowship, I was: *"Worthy of death, not by stoning, but to be cut up piece by piece, and your remains given to dogs and hyenas…"*

The letter, which came to our office by fax said that we *"should be eliminated from the face of this earth. You have the audacity to insult 2 billion adherents to this mighty and great religion, the perfect and final religion of the almighty. If you and your concoction of lies think that you can ridicule the last and final prophet of god, namely the holy prophet Muhammad (peace be upon him) without retribution from just one person of the 2 billion plus Muslim men and women of the face of this earth, then you must think again. The Fatwa will definitely come for you, sooner or later you will meet your real maker. You are worthy of death…Go burn in hell…LONG LIVE ISLAM, AMANDLA ISLAM."* (We have edited out the coarse language and vile swear words from this letter.)

EXPECT TO BE SHOT ON SIGHT

This was not the first death threat that I'd received from Muslim extremists. The official Government of Sudan, Ministry of Foreign Affairs, website posted an article *"Why Churches In Sudan Are Not Bombed"* which bluntly stated that Peter Hammond should *"expect to be bombed"* every time he comes to Sudan, he should "expect to be shot on sight". They even gave the reason: *"Because his writings make him an enemy of the state!"* We also had Muslims at the gate of our mission headquarters in Cape Town complaining about my Muslim Evangelism Workshop Manual.

All of this, taken along with the bombings and assassinations by Muslim extremists worldwide, hardly support the contention of those who say that Islam is a religion of peace and tolerance.

FREEDOM OF SPEECH UNDER FIRE

However, that a Christian Missions Week at a university can be intimidated by Muslim students is particularly disturbing. Universities are meant to be places of critical investigation. Freedom of speech is an essential foundation for any serious education. Universities must be a free market place of ideas where dissent, disagreements, debates and open discussion without threats and interference with the freedom of others is essential to discover the truth which will set us free.

FREEDOM OF RELIGION THREATENED

The TUKS Missions Week is the biggest Christian activity on the campus of Pretoria University. That threats by Muslim students should intimidate a missions committee to exclude a mission to Muslims has far reaching implications. If a university cannot protect freedom of speech, and if a missions week cannot exercise freedom of religion, without threats of violence, what are the implications for other universities and missions weeks?

I phoned the Chairperson of the Missions Committee and she informed me that the Missions Committee had no choice but to withdraw the invitation for our mission representative because: *"We were scared for his life"; "We did not want to have trouble…"; "We can't provide 24 hour security…"; "We can't have a riot on campus…"; "Your exhibitor was in danger…"; "He was threatened".*

I asked if our missionary had threatened anyone and I was told: *"No, he was the one being threatened…"* So, I asked why it is that the victim of this threat of violence was the one being excluded, instead of those students who had done the threatening?

WHO IS BEING INTOLERANT?

Then I was told that our missions literature was *"insensitive"*, that UP is a multi-racial, multi-cultural university which needed to be sensitive to the beliefs of other students. And incredibly, she declared that Christian students would have reacted in just the same way had there been similar literature written against their beliefs! To this I had to strenuously disagree. The Islamic Propagation Centre International has printed multiplied millions of copies of offensive, blasphemous, anti-Christian publications, such as *Crucifiction or*

Cruci-fiction, The God Who Never Was, etc., much of which had been distributed on the UP campus.

Despite a relentless barrage of anti-Christian publications, articles and films, I was not aware of a single case of Christians threatening violence, carrying out bombings, or assassinations, in retaliation to anti-Christian blasphemy. The most blasphemous film ever produced, *The Last Temptation of Christ*, received much protest, but again, I wasn't aware of any violence perpetrated by Christians against Universal Pictures as a result.

TOO CONTROVERSIAL

At this the chairperson agreed that she did not actually know of any cases where Christians had threatened violence, but all she meant was that it was understandable that the Muslims would be offended by our article. I pointed out to her that *The End of Islam* article was only a reaction to relentless Islamic propaganda against Christianity. Our article, and the book on which it is based, *Slavery, Terrorism and Islam - The Historical Roots and Contemporary Threat*, seeks to objectively and factually answer the relentless propaganda of Muslim publications.

At this I was informed that she and the Missions Committee *"totally agree with Frontline Fellowship, with your work and what you write..."* It was not that there was anything inaccurate that they were objecting to, but merely *"the tone"*, that it was *"too hard...too controversial..."* I had to point out that much of the Bible is also very controversial and offensive to many, but we have to love the Muslims enough to tell them the truth.

TELLING THE TRUTH IN LOVE

Basic to any missions conference is the fact that Jesus Christ is the only way to God; All other religions are false; All outside of Christ are lost and need redemption in Christ.

Muslims are the largest group of un-reached people in the world. To point out to them that there is no atonement, no forgiveness of sins, in Islam, that they need to turn in repentance from their sins and place their faith in Jesus Christ alone for salvation, may be offensive to Muslims, but it is the truth. It is also the reason why we have missions.

WHERE IS THIS GOING TO END?

If a group of non-Christians are allowed to interfere with our freedom of religion, and intimidate organisers of a missions event to exclude a mission to Muslims, where is that going to end? If every mission to Muslims is excluded from Missions Weeks, then can the Hindus not insist that missions to Hindus are similarly excluded? If those who offend the homosexuals, or any other group, can be excluded, then are Missions Weeks only to consist of those organisations which do not offend anyone? Is it possible to fulfil the Great Commission without offending some people?

BLAME THE VICTIM

Is it justice when the victims of violent threats are excluded instead of those guilty of making the violent threats? Are the victims always to blame?

TOLERATING INTOLERANCE

How effective are our universities going to be if they can tolerate such threats to freedom of speech? How effective will our Missions Weeks be if they allow Muslim militants to interfere with which missions may participate? Is this part of a larger campaign to sideline Christianity off the campuses?

THE GREAT COMMISSION IS OUR PRIORITY

I have been a missionary for 28 years. For most of that time I have specialised in Islam. By God's grace, I have had the privilege of smuggling some of the largest shipments of Bibles ever delivered into an officially Islamic country. The Frontline Fellowship mission base in Sudan was bombed ten times by the Sudan Air Force. I've come under artillery and rocket attack and aerial bombardments while preaching in churches in Sudan.

We expect opposition from militant Muslims. What we do not expect is that Christians who invited us to a Missions Week would bow so quickly to the intimidation and threats of those people who we should be committed to reaching for our Lord Jesus Christ.

"Finally, brethren, pray for us, that the Word of the Lord may run swiftly and be glorified, just as it is with you, and that we may be delivered from unreasonable and wicked men; for not all have faith."　　　　2 Thessalonians 3:1-2

Appendix XII

Islamic Attacks on Christ and the Bible
With Blasphemies, Lies And Distortions

Most Christians are unaware of a growing campaign by Muslims to undermine the integrity and trustworthiness of our Bible and to ridicule Jesus Christ, our Lord.

This began with poorly designed duplicated sheets in years past but has now escalated to a production of professionally laid-out booklets with editions of up to 100,000 copies per title. These are offered free of charge to anyone and are advertised i.a. in the media.

Some extracts of these publications are self-explanatory:

REGARDING THE BIBLE

"What used to be the Word of God has been so adulterated by human hands that the Word of God is hardly distinguishable from the word of man. In some places we do still find a glimmer of the truth that Jesus taught - the gems of divine wisdom that he uttered for the good of his people - but these are few and far between in the jungles of interpolations and contradictions with which the Bible is dense."

"It will make any reasonable man wonder how this book ever came to be called 'the Word of God'! The present Bible, therefore, can never by any stretch of imagination be called 'the inspired Word of God'."

"It is admitted by the most learned men in the Hebrew language that the present English version of the Old Testament contains at least one hundred thousand errors!" (This would amount to about 4 errors in each verse!*)

"Faith demands total allegiance to the Bible - with its faults, absurdities, everything. Reason, on the other hand, is loath to accept matters that constitute an insult to the human intelligence."

"*Although an extravagant claim is put foreward by Bible Societies and other fanatics that the Bible is the most read book in the world, the contrary is true*"

"*Paul, who had only hearsay knowledge of Jesus, provided the followers of Jesus with a religion to go with the faith they had. But he changed the teachings of Jesus and in a very serious way; a way that was guaranteed to obscure and practically replace the Message which Jesus brought to the Children of Israel, to whom he was sent by God.*"

CONCERNING JESUS

1. "*If it is possible for God to have a 'son', then why is it not possible for Him to have a grandson also? In this way He will be able to raise generations of he-gods and she-gods.*"

2. "*Why did God create Adam and fill the earth with sins? Could He not easily have raised His own family of he-gods and she-gods to dwell the earth and swell the heaven?*"

3. "*In His first experiment of creating mankind, God was a failure: 'And God saw that the wickedness of man was great in the earth, and that every imagination of the thoughts of his heart was only evil continually. AND IT REPENTED THE LORD THAT HE HAD MADE MAN ON THE EARTH, AND IT GRIEVED HIM AT HIS HEART.'(Genesis 6:5-6). So the questions are:*

   (a) *Why cannot He be a failure in His second experiment of wiping sin off from the face of the earth by hanging his only begotten son?*

   (b) *Since the son departed from this earth and is sitting snugly beside his daddy, has the sin decreased or increased? If the latter is true, then*

   (c) *Has not God failed in His second experiment as well?*"

MOCKING THE DEITY OF CHRIST

"*God*" *Was Panic-Stricken: "After these things Jesus walked in Galilee: for he would not walk in Jewry, because the Jews sought to kill him*" *(John 7:2).*

"*A Hysterical "God". "And he began to be SORE AMAZED and to be VERY HEAVY*" *(Mark 14:33),*"

"*A Weak "God": "And there appeared an angel unto him from heaven, STRENGTHENING Him*" *(Luke 22:43).*"

"The Dumb and Docile "God": "He was led as a sheep to the slaughter; and like a lamb dumb before his shearer, so opened he not his mouth" (Acts 8:32). "

"God" Was Condemned to Death: "And they all condemned him to be guilty of death" (Mark 14:64)."

"'They answered and said, He is guilty of death' (Matthew 26:66)."

"The Sabre-Rattling "God": Jesus said: "And he that hath no sword, let him sell his garment, and buy one" (Luke 22:36). "

REGARDING CHRISTIANS, THEIR FAITH, AND TEACHERS, AN ABSURD PICTURE IS PRESENTED

"The faith, therefore, as practised by present-day Christians, is a strange mixture of paganism, Paulianity and Churchianity. It has no connection at all with the dispensation brought by Jesus Christ, the holy PROPHET of God."

"Mostly, the poor fellows are mis-informed and actually ignorant, but full of what someone has called "the arrogance of ignorance". Also, they are taught to teach their beliefs, not to question them, as everyone ought to do.'

"What amazes one is that despite all their learning these "Men of God" have failed dismally to use their God-given gift of reason. And they have forbidden their congregation also, on pain of eternal damnation, to use their sense of reason."

MUSLIM'S DUTY

"We Muslims really have done nothing for the benighted millions of the world. We should rescue them from the shirk, (i.e. A theol. Arabic term implying the association of other beings with Allah. A most heinous sin in Islam) or else they will take us down with them to perdition, here as well as in the hereafter. There are many millions more worshipping man-gods today on Allah's good earth, than those worshipping the one true God - Allah subhanahu-wa-ta aala. The miseries in the Muslim world exist because of our utter neglect in sharing the Din-ul-lah (The Religion of God) with the nations of the world. Propagation of the Faith is the Awwal (the first) Fard (obligation) of the Muslim. Discount this Pillar of Islam at your own peril. You know that Allah's whip makes no noise."

(These extracts in italics are taken from: *"The Bible: Word of God or Word of Man?"* by A.S.K. Joommal. *"The Search for Truth"* by Abdur-

Rahmalan P. Wright. *"Atnatu, a novel concept of God"* by Ahmed Deedat. *"The God that Never Was"* by Ahmed Deedat. Copies of the above may be ordered from: The Islamic Propagation Centre, Madressa Arcade, Grey Street, DURBAN. 3001)

AND HOW WE CAN REACT

That such propaganda is actually whole-heartedly accepted by the overwhelming majority of Muslims is at least partly due to an almost total absence of a contextualised Christian witness to Muslims up to now.

The mode and content of these Islamic attacks betray their real author to us: the "father of lies", the devil (John 8:44).

We could submit all these publications to the Publications board. The outcome would be clear. The Publications Act No. 42 of 1974 stipulates that a publication *"shall be deemed to be undesirable if it or part of it . . . is blasphemous or is offensive to the religious convictions of any section of the inhabitants of the Republic . . ."*

As Christians we prefer to expose the content of the writings as fabricated lies and wilfull distortions and misrepresentations (Eph. 5:11) and thus to destroy these arguments (2 Cor. 10:5). We like to do this in a factual and spiritual way, presenting also the positive message of God's salvation through His only provision for mankind: Jesus Christ (Acts 4:12).

We owe this message to our Muslim friends. Their minds are already largely and deeply influenced by anti-Christian propaganda as you just read. But we also have an obligation to those men and women of Christian background, who are also subjected to this type of deceit.

We are aware that here *"we do not fight against flesh and blood"* (Eph. 6:12). In this situation we are asked by Christ, our Lord: *"How can one enter a strong man's house (Satan's realm of rule) and plunder his goods?"* The answer is given by Christ Himself: not *"unless he binds the strong man"* first! He then (Matt. 12:29-30) continues: *"He who is not with Me is against Me, and he who does not gather with Me scatters"!!!*

Therefore the whole Church, every Christian believer, is now called upon to bind the *"strong man"* so that those under his influence might be freed. Let us pledge to pray daily, faithfully, devotedly and specifically for the Muslims within our geographical reach.

But then let every Christian make sure that he or she is for Christ, which is expressed by gathering with Him! Each one of us is in touch with some Muslims - at work, in school or university, in business or in the neighbourhood. We are aware that Muslims need a somewhat specialised approach. This can be learned. The needed information or training we have specialised to provide (literature, seminars in your church, tapes, hand -out-literature etc.) Please ask us for whatever you need!

The complete tract is available from: **www.lifechallenge.de**

The Battle of Lepanto 7 October 1571 was one of the most critical naval battles in history. The destruction of the massive Turkish fleet stopped the Muslim advance and saved Europe.

Appendix XIII

Reformation Or Islamisation

"Another generation grew up, who knew neither the Lord nor what He had done...They provoked the Lord to anger." Judges 2:10 –11

EUROPE IS IN DANGER OF FALLING TO ISLAM

There is an urgent and serious need for a new Biblical Reformation and for a fresh Spiritual Revival. Only Christianity – true Biblical Christianity - can defeat radical Islam. Secular Humanism and Hedonism are no match for Islamic Jihad.

By rejecting Christianity, Europe is committing spiritual suicide.

By embracing secular Humanism and welcoming Islamic immigration, Europe is committing cultural and economic suicide. By intermarrying with Muslims and building mosques and madressas throughout the continent Europe is betraying future generations to bondage. The decline of Christianity in Europe is catastrophic.

History is repeating itself. Like in the 15th and 16th Centuries, Europe is experiencing a renaissance of paganism and facing an aggressive Islamic expansionism that threatens Faith and freedom. Those who forget the lessons of history are doomed to repeat its failures. Guilt manipulation and Revisionism has neutralized Europe. We need to rediscover our history. As Karl Marx declared: *"The first battlefield is the re-writing of history."*

As Alexander Solzenitzen declared, of Russia, in 1917: **"We forgot God!"**

Secularism, Humanism, Hedonism and Heathenism have gutted Europe – morally, spiritually and ethically – making it vulnerable to an Islamic takeover.

The book of Judges tells us of *"another generation"* which *"grew up, who knew neither the Lord nor what He had done"* (Judges 2:10). We now have a secular society which has rejected the pleasure of worship and replaced it with the worship of pleasure.

Europe has a new generation who have moved away from the rock certainties of Biblical Christianity to the sands of relativism, evolutionism, situational ethics, relative truth, reincarnation, *Harry Potter, The Da Vinci Code* Hoax, *The Gospel of Judas* and the occult. Like Esau, they have sold their birthright for a mess of pottage. Now young Europeans are taught: *"You come from nothing, You're going nowhere, life is meaningless!"*

> ***"These are the nations the Lord left to test all those Israelites who had not experienced any of the wars in Canaan (He did this only to teach warfare to the descendants of the Israelites who had not had previous battle experience)...They were left to test the Israelites to see whether they would obey the Lord's Commands..."***
>
> Judges 3:1 – 2

THE BLESSINGS OF THE GOSPEL

From the time of the Reformation, Europe became the world's dominant industrial region. The productivity and innovations of Europe brought blessings to the whole world:

📖 **Medical science** that saved lives and extended life expectancy worldwide;

📖 **Agricultural productivity**, which increased from the wooden plough feeding one family, to the iron plough feeding 3 families, to the tractor feeding 60 families. Europe's agricultural innovations ended famines;

📖 **Missionaries** brought the blessings of literacy, education and the Gospel of Christ to nations which had never before even had a written language;

📖 **Democratic forms of government and the rule of law;**

📖 **The abolition of slavery** and the slave trade, setting the captives free;

📖 **Roads, railways, bridges, schools, hospitals, law courts, churches, the Bible** in hundreds of previously unwritten languages.

All of these blessings, and much, much more, God provided through previous generations of Europeans – who were faithful to God's Word and faithful to God's Work. Never, in all of history has any continent blessed so many millions worldwide as Europe has done – through the Reformation and the great missionary movements.

ANOTHER GENERATION

But now *"another generation"* has grown up *"who know neither the Lord, nor what He has done…"* Instead of building on the solid rock of God's Word, many Europeans today are building on the sand of Humanism, Evolutionism and Hedonism.

Europe is living on borrowed blessings. Like a cut flower the beauty can only abide for a short time – because it is cut off from the source of its life. Soon the petals will fade and crumble and only the thorns will remain.

By abandoning its Christian roots and missionary calling, Europe is cutting itself off from the very source of its blessings, freedom, productivity and prosperity. It is of great concern to us Africans that while many millions of Africans are turning to Christ, millions of Europeans are turning their backs on Christ. While we are rejecting heathenism and embracing Christ, Europe is rejecting Christ and embracing heathenism.

"They exchanged the truth of God for a lie..."   Romans 1:25

Another generation" has arisen that neither knows the Lord personally, nor even knows about their great Christian heritage and what God has done in, with and through Europe. What Alexander Solzenitzen said of Russia on the eve of the Communist takeover/Revolution in Russia in 1917 can be said of most of Europe today in 2006: *"THEY FORGOT GOD!"*

> *"For although they knew God, they neither glorified Him as God, nor gave thanks to Him, but their thinking became futile and their foolish hearts were darkened."*
>
> Romans 1:21

They took God's blessings for granted and did not acknowledge Him. They neglected God's Holy Word, the Bible – the very Book which has been the foundation and fountain of all their freedoms, productivity, prosperity and blessings.

ABORTING EUROPE
- By aborting her babies, Europe is aborting her future.
- By secularising her schools, Europe is condemning her youth.
- By paganising her population, Europe is perverting her society.
- By importing millions of Muslim migrant workers, Europe is committing suicide.

THE TURKISH CONNECTION
Turkey, which once threatened all of Europe, is now considered for European Union membership. In 1453, when Constantinople was the greatest city in the world, the Turks massacred its entire population. When the *Hagia Sophia* was the greatest church building in the world the Turks slaughtered the entire congregation, men, women and children, young and old. In 1526, the Turks conquered Budapest and looted the

city. They then enslaved 200,000 Hungarian Christians and dragged them back to Turkey as slaves. Vienna itself was besieged by the Turks in the 16 th and 17 th Centuries – even as late as 1683.

What is today *Turkey* was once the Christian Byzantine Empire – The land of the Seven Churches of Revelation. The Turks invaded and overwhelmed the Christians of the Byzantine Empire and eradicated the Christians until they were a minority in their own lands. Finally in 1915 the Turks exterminated the Christian minority – the Armenians. 1,5 million Christian Armenians were massacred by the Turks. As recently as 1922 the last Christian city in Asia, Smyrna, was destroyed by the Turks. A city of 300,000 people wiped out. The Biblical city of Smyrna, where the Apostle John had ministered, annihilated by the Turkish army, in living memory. And now some are considering welcoming Turkey into the EU.

EURABIA

Studying the history of Islam and Europe I am convinced that should Muslims attain a majority in any country in Europe – they would similarly oppress, persecute, eliminate and ultimately exterminate all Christian minorities within their control. Muslims are openly talking about turning Europe into Eurabia.

Moammar Gadhafi of Libya has claimed on Al Jazeera television (10 April 2006): *"We have 50 million Muslims in Europe. There are signs that Allah will grant Islam victory in Europe…within a few decades."* Gadhafi pointed out that already Albania and Bosnia with Muslim majorities have entered the European Union. If Turkey is added to the EU, Europe will have another 50 million Muslims. Gaddafi exclaimed: Muhammad *"superseded all previous religions. If Jesus were alive when Muhammad was sent, he would have followed him. All people must be Muslim!"*

We need to rediscover our history. And we need to understand the signs of the times. Europe has faced a similar threat of radical, violent, Islamic expansionism before, in the 16th Century. And Europe experienced a similar renaissance of paganism before. In the 15th

Century. The threat is the same. And the solution is the same today as it was then. **We need Reformation!**

Do you understand the threat of Islam? The reality of Sharia law?

EUROPE IS BEING TARGETED BY ISLAM

Recent intelligence reports include the following disturbing facts:

- **FRANCE:** 1945 there were 100,000 Muslims in France, today it is officially claimed to be 6 million (60 x increase), 10% of the population. But Muslims make up 70% of France's convicted criminals in prison. Of the over 1,000 Muslim neighbourhoods in France, 700 are listed as "violent", 400 "very violent". There are 1,000 mosques in France. In France 95% of convicted rapists are Muslims, 85% of convicted murderers are Muslims, and 58% of convicted thieves are Muslims.

- **HOLLAND:** Muslims are officially 15% of population.

- **BELGIUM:** 10% of population. Half of all babies born in Belgium are now Muslims.

- **GERMANY:** 2 million Muslims (Berlin has the 4th largest Turkish population in the world.)

- **BRITAIN:** 2 million (from 82,000 – 30 years ago - x 25 increase) British counter-terrorism experts estimate that there are up to 25,000 Al-Qaeda supporters in UK. 1,000 Mosques in Britain.

- **SWEDEN:** 400,000 Muslims. Massive increase in attacks on Jewish population in Sweden.

- **DENMARK:** 200,000 Muslim immigrants are trying to dictate their anti-Israel, Anti-American policies to the 5 million Danes. Although Muslims are only 4% of the population, they consume over 40% of the social welfare spending. They also make up 75% of the country's convicted rapists.

- **ITALY:** 1 million Muslims (In Italy Muslims make up 95% of all convicted rapists and 85% of all convicted murderers.)

Note that of 48 countries with a Muslim majority – 46 are dictatorships.

The Saudi Arabian government has financed the building of 1,500 mosques, 210 Islamic centers, 202 colleges and 2,000 madressas (Islamic Quranic schools) in non-Muslim countries – mostly in Europe.

Security experts estimate that 5% of the 18 million Muslims now living in Europe are radical terrorist supporters and sympathizers, representing at least 75,000 to 90,000 potential terrorists within Europe's borders.

And while the average European woman has 1.5 children the average Muslim woman in Europe has 6 to 8 children.

REJECTING GOD'S LAW
By rejecting God's Law, France may soon fall under Islamic Sharia law! It started with the St. Bartholomew's Day Massacre in 1572 and the vicious persecution of the French Hugenots (the Protestants). Then with King Louis XIV's Revocation of the Edict of Nantes in 1685 when all Protestants were stripped of their rights and forced to flee France. Within a century the French Revolution slaughtered tens of thousands on the guillotine. Now France faces an Islamic Revolution. By rejecting God's Law they are heading for Islamic Sharia law.

ABORTING HER FUTURE
A recent report published in Christian News by CFT warned that Europe is dying by failure to have enough children. Patrick Buchanan in *"The Death of The West"* projected that, if present trends continue, by the end of the century, Europe's indigenous population will have plummeted from 728 million to 207 million.

Gene Veith of World notes: *"Thanks to contraceptive technology, sex has become separated from child bearing. With women pursuing careers of their own and men getting sex without the responsibility of marriage, why bother with children? For many women and men, pregnancy has become an unpleasant side effect, something to prevent with contraceptives or easily treated with a trip to the abortion clinic."*

Christian News from CFT quotes Allan Carlson as saying: *"A pervasive hedonism...permeates the West...What's ironic however is that this pursuit of personal pleasure and wealth may result in economic ruin.* " Veith lists some of the disastrous consequences of population decline: *"Citizens are not just consumers, but producers. Having fewer people can wreak havoc on an economy, creating both a labour shortage and a shortage of buyers. A government with a shrinking population faces a smaller military and fewer taxpayers. Dwindling populations have always signaled cultural decline, with less creativity, energy and vitality on every level of society."*

"The great party of Western hedonism will not last much longer. There is an iron law in history: **the future belongs to the fertile.** *Just as the clan centred, child rich Barbarian tribes of the Germans swept away the sensuous and sterile Western Roman Empire, so shall new barbarians arise."*

By abandoning its Christian heritage, aborting its babies, embracing hedonism and perversion, demanding unlimited personal freedoms, Europe is heading towards the repression of Islamic Sharia law. By rejecting Christianity, Europe is in danger of falling under Islamic totalitarianism.

The combined effects of affluence and a rapidly falling birthrate have made Western Europe a magnet for millions of impoverished Muslims from North Africa and the Middle East. And with most Europeans embracing a practical atheism or a fuzzy new age spirituality, they are incapable of comprehending, let alone effectively dealing with, radical Islam. That, in a nutshell, is the problem.

WHAT IS THE SOLUTION?

How are we as Christians to respond to this serious threat to faith and freedom in Europe? How can we be MORE THAN CONQUERERS in this crisis?

We need to **recognise**

- **God's enemies**: Secular Humanism and Radical Islam.
- **God's weapons**: Bible teaching, Evangelism, Prayer – including the Imprecatory Psalms.
- **God's Battle plan/strategy**: The Great Commission, God-fearing families and discipleship.

There are **two extremes we need to guard against:** There are those who refuse to see the crisis. They say there is NO PROBLEM! Then there are those who panic and say that there is NO HOPE!

We must **recognise the problems** – honestly and soberly. Man is depraved and in rebellion to God and His Word. Sin inevitably reaps tremendous trouble. But we must also recognise that God is Sovereign and Almighty, there is power in prayer, and the Gospel is the power of God for the salvation of all who believe. How can any Christian say that there is "no hope!"?

We must **wake up to the urgent and serious crisis.** Most churches are asleep or in apostasy. The world is rushing by on its way to hell, and yet our prayer meetings are sparsely attended and lacking in fire and fervor. Most evangelical churches engage in very little or no evangelism. Missionary vision is weak and much that is done in the name of "missions" has little to do with fulfilling the Great Commission, "making disciples …teaching obedience…" To use some military terminology: Most of the Christian Army in Europe is either on AWOL (absent without leave) or conscientious objectors. The few faithful are often content to sing in the barracks instead of engaging the enemy on the battlefield.

But we are called to conquest. We must not merely survive – we need to **thrive.** We are called to be **MORE THAN CONQUERERS.**

- **We must conquer fear.** *"God has not given us a spirit of fear – but of power and of love and of a sound mind."* 2 Timothy 1:7
- **We must conquer cowardice.** *"Be strong in the Lord and in the power of His might. Put on the whole armour of God, that you may be able to stand against the wiles of the devil."* Ephesians 6:10 – 11
- **We must conquer ignorance.** *"My people are destroyed from lack of knowledge."* Hosea 4:6
- **We must conquer unbelief.** We must *"overcome the world"* by our faith (1 John 5:4).

WHO IS ON THE LORD'S SIDE?

"Choose for yourselves this day whom you will serve."

Joshua 24:15

There has never been a more urgent need for Biblical Reformation than now. Our Faith, our Freedoms and our Families are at stake.

"For the eyes of the Lord range throughout the earth to strengthen those whose hearts are fully committed to Him." 2 Chronicles 16:9

We need the Faith and courage of Martin Luther, who could stand before the assembled might of Europe and declare: *"My conscience is captive to the Word of God! Here I stand. I can do no other. So help me God. Amen."*

We need the courage and conviction of Ulrich Zwingli who declared: *"They can kill the body – but not the soul!"*

We need the doctrine and devotion of John Calvin whose motto was *"promptly and sincerely in the service of my God."*

We need to be more courageous, more faithful and more effective in fulfilling the Great Commission. Humanism is self-destructive. Islam's days are numbered. Islam cannot survive freedom and the Quran cannot withstand critical academic scrutiny.

We must win our enemies to Christ – David was a conqueror because he killed Goliath. Jesus Christ was more than a conqueror because he turned Saul the persecutor of the church into Paul the great Apostle of the church. We are called to be more than conquerors. We must understand Islam and we must evangelise Muslims.

"Every knee shall bow, every tongue confess that Jesus Christ is Lord." Phillipians 2:10 – 11

"The earth will be filled with the knowledge of the glory of the Lord as the waters cover the sea." Habakkuk 2:14

As Charles Martel – "The Hammer" – stopped the Muslim advance at the Battle of Tours, 732 AD, we need to rouse the church to evangelise our Muslim neighbours and to stop the Muslim advance in Europe. As Christians liberated Romania, Hungary, Bulgaria and Greece from centuries of oppression by the Turks so we need to free our neighbours from the deception of Islam and lead them to Christ.

Let us rediscover our history and heritage. As Luther utilized the printing press to mobilise the Reformation so we need to use DTP, the Internet, CDs, DVDs, MP3s, radio, websites and well-illustrated books to advance the Gospel today. Europe must be won back to Christ. And Africa needs a Biblical Reformation and a spiritual Revival. Africa for Christ!

"Restore us, O God Almighty; make Your face shine upon us, that we may be saved."　　　　　　　　　　Psalm 80:7

It is either: GOD'S LAW or SHARIA LAW
CHRISTIANITY or ISLAM
REFORMATION or ISLAMISATION
Let us wake up and get back to the Bible.
Fear God alone and love God wholeheartedly.
Let us work and pray for Reformation and Revival.
We must be more than conquerors and win our nations back to Christ.

"Will You not revive us again, that Your people may rejoice in You?"　　　　　　　　　　Psalm 85:6

Bibliography

A History of Christianity, by Kenneth Scott Latourette, Harper, 1953

Calvin on Islam, by Dr. Francis Nigel Lee , Lamp Trimmers, El Paso, Texas 2000.

Christian Slaves, Muslim Masters: White Slavery in the Mediterranean; the Barbary Coast and Italy 1500 - 1800, by Robert Davis, Palgrave MacMillan, 2004

God's Politician, by Garth Lean, Helmers and Howard, 1987

History of Slavery, by Suzanne Everett, Chartwell, 1997

Islam - As it Sees Itself, As Others See It, As it Is, by Gerhard Nehls and Walter Eric, Life Challenge Africa / SIM, 1996

Islam's Black Slaves, by Ronald Segal, Farrar, New York, 2001

Millat-a-Ibrahim: The True Faith Of Abraham by John Gilchrist

Missionary Travels and Researches in South Africa, by David Livingstone, London, 1857

Narrative of an Expedition to the Zambezi, by David Livingstone, London,1865

Reach Out – a Guide to Muslim Evangelism" by Gerhard Nehls and Walter Eric (Life Challenge Africa/SIM).

Secrets of the Koran, by Don Richardson, Regal, 2003

The Blood of the Moon , by George Grant, Wolgemuth and Hyatt, 1991

The Crusades - A History, by Jonathan Riley-Smith, Yale University, 2005

The Greatest Century of Missions, by Peter Hammond, CLB, 2002

The Islamic Invasion, by Robert Morey, Christian Scholars Press, 1992

The Life of Muhammad, by William Muir, T & T Clark, 1923

The Slave Trade, by Hugh Thomas, 1997

The Sword of the Prophet, by Serge Trifkovic, Regina Orthodox Press, 2002

Under the Influence - How Christianity Transformed Civilization, by Alvin Schmit, Zondervan, 2001

Why I am not a Muslim, by Ibn Warraq, Prometheus Books, 1995

Websites on Islam:

www.answering-islam.org

www.armenian-genocide.org

www.debate.org.uk

www.faithdefenders.com

www.frontline.org.za

www.genocide1915.info

www.lifechallenge.de

END NOTES

Chapter 4: **Jihad - Islamic Holy War** - Notes

1. World Vision Magazine, August 1978.
2. Islam on the March, Africa Now, SIM, 1978.
3. World Vision, August 1978.
4. "The Holy Quran – a Message from the Lord of the Worlds." – M.S. Laher, Islamic Missionary Society, pages 1, 2 & 3.
5. "The Holy Quran – a Message from the Lord of the Worlds." – M.S. Laher, Islamic Missionary Society, pages 1, 2 & 3.
6. Dictionary of Islam, T.P. Hughes, pg.. 515.
7. Understanding the Islamic Explosion, Bernard Palmer, pg. 94.
8. Christians Ask Muslims, Gehard Nehls, pg. 96.
9. Ibid, pg. 97.
10. Understanding the Islamic Explosion, Palmer, pg. 94.
11. Christians Ask Muslims, Nehls, pg. 97.
12. The Sources of Islam, Rev. W. St. Clair – Tisdall, pg. 12.
13. Ibid, pg. 40.
14. The Sources of Islam, Clair – Tisdall, pg. 14-16.
15. Ibid, pg. 16-24.
16. The Sources of Islam, Clair-Tisdall, pg. 24-30.
17. Ibid. pg. 30-36.
18. Islam, Alfred Guillaume, pg. 62.
19. Christians Ask Muslims, Nehls, pg. 98.
20. Ibid, pg. 98.
21. The World's Religions, Sir Norman, Anderson, pg. 52
22. Understanding the Islamic Explosion, Palmer, pg. 94.
23. Christ in Islam, Ahmed Deedat, pg. 2.
24. Sources of Islam, Clair-Tisdall, pg. 55 & 56.
25. Ibid, pg. 58.
26. Ibid, pg. 57.
27. Ibid, pg. 62.

28. Christians ask Muslims, Nehls, pg. 99.
29. The Sources of Islam, Clair-Tisdall, pg. 49-50.
30. Ibid, pg. 52-55.
31. Ibid, pg. 47-48.
32. The Sources of Islam, Clair-Tisdall, pg. 47-48.
33. Christians ask Muslims, Nehls, pg. 7.
34. Ibid, pg. 8.
35. Ibid, pg. 100.
36. Christians ask Muslims, Nehls, pg. 101.

Chapter 6: **The Sources of Islam** - Notes

1. World Vision Magazine, August 1978.
2. Islam on the March, Africa Now, SIM, 1978.
3. World Vision, August 1978.
4. "The Holy Quran – a Message from the Lord of the Worlds."
   – M.S. Laher, Islamic Missionary Society, pages 1, 2 & 3.
5. "The Holy Quran – a Message from the Lord of the Worlds."
   – M.S. Laher, Islamic Missionary Society, pages 1, 2 & 3.
6. Dictionary of Islam, T.P. Hughes, pg.. 515.
7. Understanding the Islamic Explosion,
   Bernard Palmer, pg. 94.
8. Christians Ask Muslims, Gehard Nehls, pg. 96.
9. Ibid, pg. 97.
10. Understanding the Islamic Explosion, Palmer, pg. 94.
11. Christians Ask Muslims, Nehls, pg. 97.
12. The Sources of Islam, Rev. W. St. Clair – Tisdall, pg. 12.
13. Ibid, pg. 40.
14. The Sources of Islam, Clair – Tisdall, pg. 14-16.
15. Ibid, pg. 16-24.
16. The Sources of Islam, Clair-Tisdall, pg. 24-30.

17. Ibid. pg. 30-36.
18. Islam, Alfred Guillaume, pg. 62.
19. Christians Ask Muslims, Nehls, pg. 98.
20. Ibid, pg. 98.
21. The World's Religions, Sir Norman Anderson, pg. 52
22. Understanding the Islamic Explosion, Palmer, pg. 94.
23. Christ in Islam, Ahmed Deedat, pg. 2.
24. Sources of Islam, Clair-Tisdall, pg. 55 & 56.
25. Ibid, pg. 58.
26. Ibid, pg. 57.
27. Ibid, pg. 62.
28. Christians ask Muslims, Nehls, pg. 99.
29. The Sources of Islam, Clair-Tisdall, pg. 49-50.
30. Ibid, pg. 52-55.
31. Ibid, pg. 47-48.
32. The Sources of Islam, Clair-Tisdall, pg. 47-48.
33. Christians ask Muslims, Nehls, pg. 7.
34. Ibid, pg. 8.
35. Ibid, pg. 100.
36. Christians ask Muslims, Nehls, pg. 101.
37. Sources of Islam, Clair-Tisdall, pg. 84, 85.
38. The World's Religions, Anderson, pg. 55.
39. Mishkat 4, pg. 354.
40. Christians ask Muslims, Nehls, pg. 44.
41. Ibid.

Other Publications Available

Other Publications Available from Frontline Fellowship
Biblical Principles for Africa (Also Available in Afrikaans and French)
Biblical Worldview Manual
Character Assassins - Dealing with Ecclesiastical Tyrants and Terrorists
David Livingstone - Man of Prayer and Action
Discipleship Handbook
Faith Under Fire in Sudan
Fight For Life - a Pro-Life Handbook for Southern Africa
Finding Freedom from the Pornography Plague
Going Through ... Even if the Door is Closed
Great Commission Manual
Greatest Century of Missions
Greatest Century of Reformation
Holocaust in Rwanda (also translated into French)
In the Killing Fields of Mozambique
Make a Difference - a Christian Action Handbook for Southern Africa
Pratical Discipleship
Putting Feet to Your Faith
Reforming our Families
South Africa - Renaissance or Reformation?
Security and Survival in Unstable Times
Shooting Back - The Right and Duty of Self-Defence
The Apostles Creed - Firm Foundations for Your Faith
The Christian at War (also translated into Spanish, German and Afrikaans)
The Christian Voice of Southern Africa
The Doctor Comes to Lui
The Ten Commandments - God's Perfect Law of Liberty
The Pink Agenda - Sexual Revolution and The Ruin of the Family
The Power of Prayer Handbook
War Against God

Audio CDs, DVDs, MP3s and Data CDs
The Biblical Worldview Summit
The Great Commission Course
Muslim Evangelism Workshop
Reformation and Revival Lectures from The Reformation Society
Life Changing Sermons from Livingstone Fellowship

FRONTLINE FELLOWSHIP

PO Box 74, Newlands 7725
Cape Town, South Africa
Tel: (+27 -21) 689 4480
Fax: (+27 -21) 685 5884
Email: admin@frontline.co.za
Web: www.frontline.org.za

FRONTLINE FELLOWSHIP - USA

Email: info@frontlinefellowship.net
Web: www.frontlinefellowship.net

BIOGRAPHICAL NOTES

Dr. Peter Hammond has been a missionary to restricted access areas for over 28 years. He has pioneered missionary outreaches into the war zones of Mozambique, Angola and Sudan. During the war in Sudan he flew far behind enemy lines to the beleaguered Nuba Mountains with tonnes of Bibles, school books, agricultural tools and seed and other relief aid. Peter has walked throughout the war devastated Nuba Mountains - an island of Christianity in a sea of Islam - showing the *Jesus* film in Arabic, proclaiming the Gospel, training pastors and evading enemy patrols.

Rev. Peter Hammond has come under aerial and artillery bombardments while preaching in churches in Sudan. The official Government of Sudan, Ministry of Foreign Affairs, website even posted an article which stated that *"Hammond should expect to be bombed in Sudan…he should expect to be shot on sight…his writings make him an enemy of the state!"* The publication of a history book on Slavery, Terrorism and Islam earned him a *fatwa* (death threat) from some Islamic radicals.

Peter delivered some of the largest shipments of Bibles ever flown into an officially Islamic state. He has conducted door to door evangelism in Muslim areas and engaged in numerous public debates with Muslim leaders - including Ahmed Deedat of the Islamic Propagation Centre International - and in mosques, including in the largest mosque in the Southern Hemisphere, in Durban. He has also been interviewed on Muslim radio stations and conducted Muslim Evangelism Workshops in Nigeria and Sudan.

Peter designed the **Great Commission Course** and the **Muslim Evangelism Workshop** to prepare and equip Christians to effectively evangelise Muslims.

Dr. Peter Hammond is the Founder and Director of Frontline Fellowship and the author of, amongst others: ***Faith Under Fire in Sudan***; ***Holocaust in Rwanda***; ***In the Killing Fields of Mozambique***; ***Putting Feet to Your Faith***; ***The Greatest Century of Missions***; ***Biblical Principles for Africa***; ***Character Assassins,*** the ***Discipleship Handbook, The Greatest Century of Reformation, The Power of Prayer Handbook, The Ten Commandments - God's Perfect Law of Liberty*** and a co-author of ***Reforming Our Families***. He is also the Editor of **Frontline Fellowship News** and **Christian Action**.

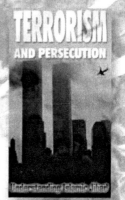

UNDERSTAND ISLAM - EVANGELISE MUSLIMS

The new, expanded edition of *Slavery, Terrorism and Islam – the Historical Roots and Contemporary Threat* has received much interest and positive responses from all over the world.

One review from an American authority states: "*Slavery, Terrorism and Islam is an invaluable desk reference and primer for analysts addressing Islam as an ideological force... unlike the academics who debate that a clash of civilisations is even in progress, Hammond writes from the perspective of one decisively engaged in that civilisational fight...*"

Dr. Peter Hammond's new book: *SLAVERY, TERRORISM & ISLAM - The Historical Roots and Contemporary Threat* is a fascinating, well illustrated and thoroughly documented response to the relentless anti-Christian propaganda that has been generated by Muslim and Marxist groups and by Hollywood film makers. As Karl Marx declared: "*The first battlefield is the re-writing of History!*"

by Peter Hammond
Foreword by George Grant

**276 Pages
220 pictures,
maps and
charts
$14**

Slavery, Terrorism and Islam was first published in 2005 and quickly sold out. It earned Dr. Peter Hammond a death threat "Fatwa" from some Islamic radicals. Now completely revised and greatly expanded, this best selling book is much in demand.

**12 Disc boxset
with audio Lectures
and Powerpoints
$30**

Our audio-visual department has also produced a Muslim Evangelism MP3 with 13 lectures and PowerPoints, a *Muslim Evangelism Workshop* 12-CD Box Set and a number of supplementary DVDs, including *Terrorism and Persecution - Understanding Islamic Jihad*. *Slavery, Terrorism & Islam* sets the record straight with chapters on "*Muhammad, the Caliphas and Jihad*", "*The Oppression of Women in Islam*", "*The Sources of Islam*" and "*Slavery the Rest of the Story*". With over 200 pictures and 15 maps and charts, this book is richly illustrated. It consists of 16 chapters and 13 very helpful appendixes including demographic maps of the spread of Islam, a Glossary of Islamic Terms, a comparison of Muslim nations' military spending vs. their national prosperity, a chart on how Jihad works depending on the percentage of Muslims in the population and guidelines for Muslim evangelism.

Breinigsville, PA USA
10 February 2011
255305BV00002B/2/P